SpringerBriefs in Computer Science

SpringerBriefs present concise summaries of cutting-edge research and practical applications across a wide spectrum of fields. Featuring compact volumes of 50 to 125 pages, the series covers a range of content from professional to academic.

Typical topics might include:

- A timely report of state-of-the art analytical techniques
- A bridge between new research results, as published in journal articles, and a contextual literature review
- A snapshot of a hot or emerging topic
- An in-depth case study or clinical example
- A presentation of core concepts that students must understand in order to make independent contributions

Briefs allow authors to present their ideas and readers to absorb them with minimal time investment. Briefs will be published as part of Springer's eBook collection, with millions of users worldwide. In addition, Briefs will be available for individual print and electronic purchase. Briefs are characterized by fast, global electronic dissemination, standard publishing contracts, easy-to-use manuscript preparation and formatting guidelines, and expedited production schedules. We aim for publication 8–12 weeks after acceptance. Both solicited and unsolicited manuscripts are considered for publication in this series.

**Indexing: This series is indexed in Scopus, Ei-Compendex, and zbMATH **

Mohammad Amin Kuhail · Jose Berengueres ·
Fatma Taher · Mariam Al Kuwaiti

Advances, Applications and the Future of Haptic Technology

Springer

Mohammad Amin Kuhail
Zayed University
Abu Dhabi, United Arab Emirates

Jose Berengueres
KTH Royal Institute of Technology
Stockholm, Sweden

Fatma Taher
Zayed University
Dubai, United Arab Emirates

Mariam Al Kuwaiti
United Arab Emirates University
Al Ain, United Arab Emirates

ISSN 2191-5768   ISSN 2191-5776 (electronic)
SpringerBriefs in Computer Science
ISBN 978-3-031-70587-8   ISBN 978-3-031-70588-5 (eBook)
https://doi.org/10.1007/978-3-031-70588-5

This Springer imprint is published by the registered company Springer Nature Switzerland AG
The registered company address is: Gewerbestrasse 11, 6330 Cham, Switzerland

If disposing of this product, please recycle the paper.

Contents

Chapter 1
Introduction

Abstract This chapter introduces the reader to haptics, a field that has enriched how we interact with the digital world through the sense of touch. This chapter defines the term and the corresponding technology, and then provides a thorough list of types of haptics organized by Physical Principle and by User Action. It also explores the historical context in which the first haptic systems emerged and discusses recent key advancements in the field. In addition, it details how haptic technology is used in healthcare, gaming, and space exploration. The chapter also discusses the challenges of applying haptics to consumer products and industrial applications to offer the reader a nuanced perspective of the technology and its cost and benefits. Finally, the chapter provides an overview of the six chapters in the book.

Keywords Haptics · Definition · Types · Drivers

1.1 Introduction to Haptic Technology

The term "haptics" is derived from the Greek word "haptein," signifying "contact" or "to touch" [1]. The perceptual system of haptics relies on a combination of sensory feedback from cutaneous (skin) and kinesthetic (muscles, tendons, and joints) inputs [2]. Thus, haptic technology provides tangible feedback by applying forces, sensations, or motions to the user, enabling a sense of touch in virtual environments [3]. Generally speaking, a system is said to be haptic when information is transmitted to the brain through the sense of touch [4]. This sensing usually begins at the skin's touch receptors. These sensors react to stimuli by sending signals to the brain through the human nervous system [5]. On the cognitive side (sense-making), the brain interprets the signals for further action [6]. However, there are instances where signals are processed locally, at the spinal cord level, often without direct involvement of the brain [7]. This is often seen in reflexive actions, quick responses to stimuli that bypass the brain [8], such as withdrawing your hand from something hot.

Commercially, haptic systems are used in a wide range of products and services, including healthcare, gaming, and consumer electronics [9]. As a technology, haptics integrates principles from engineering, computer science, human perception, physics, and information technology [10]. Haptic technology also applies to user experience design (UX). Companies such as Apple and Nintendo have provided developers with interfaces to high-fidelity inertial actuators in their devices [11], while startups such as Tanvas and UltraLeap are adopting new technologies such as programmable friction [12, 13] and mid-air haptics, aka metasurfaces [14].

Haptic technology gives individuals feedback on how much their limbs are moving and how much force they exert. This feedback enables individuals to perform tasks more effectively [15]. For example, when an individual types on a smartphone's virtual keyboard, it typically emits a slight vibration to replicate the sensation of striking a physical key [16]. This stimulus is generated by a haptic actuator, also known as a linear resonant actuator (LRA).

Haptics can also mimic various features of the sense of touch, giving users direct sensory feedback that makes it easier to connect with digital or remote settings. Two main methods to mimic the sense of touch are force and vibration. The first method generates a force on the user that can be adjusted to simulate any parameter (mass, acceleration) of Newton's second law of motion ($F = ma$) [17]. The second method uses oscillation to create a vibration on the skin. This method can mimic the vibrations on the skin when fingers slide through textured surfaces, the feel of a 'click,' and other stimuli [18]. Since the 1990s (see Chap. 5), vibration has become prevalent in consumer electronics such as mobile phones, as it enhances user interaction with such devices [19]. The predominant actuator of choice in consumer electronics is the excentric mass attached to a DC motor and the more powerful LRAs used in Apple laptops and Sony remote controls. However, alternative methods of haptic actuating principles exist, such as airflow and thermal input [20, 21].

Given the interest and utility of haptic technology, this chapter aims to introduce the reader to the technology by providing historical context for the technology (Sect. 1.2), an overview of haptic feedback systems and types (Sect. 1.3), a summary of the key drivers of the haptic industry (Sect. 1.4), and an overview of the technology's applications and challenges (Sects. 1.5 and 1.6). Finally, we provide an overview of the book (Sect. 1.7) and conclude the chapter.

1.2   Historical Context of Haptics

Understanding the historical evolution of haptics from both physiological and technical perspectives is crucial to developing haptic technology. From a physiological perspective, Ernst Heinrich Weber was among the first physiologists to systematically investigate the sense of touch in the nineteenth century [22]. His pioneering study established the basis for understanding the physiology of haptic perception. His understanding of haptics involved identifying highly sensitive skin patches known as "sensorial circles" and developing the law of just-noticeable changes. Max von Frey's subsequent study expanded on haptic awareness by establishing the presence of pain sites [23]. The pain sites revealed the presence of particular organs responsible for various feelings, such as pressure, temperature, coolness, and pain. Undoubtedly, this basic understanding of haptics has moved us a step in the direction of haptic systems.

One of the earliest attempts at developing haptic interfaces was the GROPE1, developed in 1967 [24]. The interface used a 2D moveable platform to simulate virtual surroundings. Subsequently, haptic interfaces such as the Argonne ARM and GROPE-III feature force feedback in activities such as molecular docking. This feedback allows researchers to feel the attractive and repulsive forces between molecules, providing a more intuitive understanding of the docking process. Building on this invention, in 1994, the Aura Interactor vest was invented, a wearable force-feedback technology that converts bass sound waves into vibrations, simulating actions such as punches or kicks [25]. Moreover, [26] pioneered a sandpaper system that enables the feeling of textures using motor-driven joysticks by creating virtual springs that respond to a texture's depth map. These springs pull the user's hand towards low regions (smooth surfaces) and away from high regions (raised areas). This invention laid the foundation for haptic rendering theory. Concurrently, this research led to the development of pend-based forced display [27], the first exoskeleton designed for haptic interaction in virtual environments. The pen-based force display system offers a familiar way (like using a pen) to precisely manipulate objects in virtual environments, even for delicate tasks like microsurgery. It works by mimicking a pen interface, where the user interacts with forces relayed through a handheld device with built-in actuators. These actuators provide resistance or assistance, creating a natural feeling for precise control. Inventions such as pen-based force displays and object-oriented haptic interfaces broadened the scope of haptic interactions [28].

In addition to these developments, early research by Dr. Raymond Goertz at the Argonne National Laboratory played a crucial role in shaping the field of haptics [29]. His pioneering work initially focused on mechanical manipulators for handling radioactive devices. This research later included electrically connected manipulators, establishing the concept of remote control and bilateral motion. This groundwork laid the foundation for modern haptics, which now includes the artificial communication of tactile and force sensations. This is particularly evident in machines capable of remote operation with precise positioning and force feedback [30]. In sum, these key advancements in haptic technology have set the stage for a wide range of future developments.

1.3 Haptic Classifications by Physical Principle and User Action

The human sense of touch can be stimulated via various physical phenomena: forces, vibration detectable by several of the tactile receptors in the human skin, stimulation of the thermal receptors in the skin, stimulation of susceptible receptors with airflow or ultrasound waves, or circumventing the tactile receptors and directly stimulating the nerves or muscles.

Human skin contains two main types of mechanoreceptors: slow-adapting and fast-adapting. Slow-adapting receptors respond to continuous stimuli such as pressure and skin stretch. Fast-adapting receptors react reflexively to stimuli like vibration [31]. Consequently, developing a comprehensive human haptic perception system requires the need to stimulate multiple types of mechanical and tactile receptors simultaneously [32]. Such a system must include thermal receptors for temperature perception, nociceptors for pain perception, and mechanoreceptors for sensing mechanical actions such as force, vibration, and pressure. These receptors work cooperatively to form tactile-kinesthetic action, providing information about spatial and physical properties of the environment, such as texture, mass, direction, distance, shape, and size [33]. Figure 1.1 depicts the shows the haptic interaction system in the human body.

Now, let's explore the details of the types of feedback by stimulation.

1. *Force:* This kind of haptic device provides mechanical stimulation to users by applying force to their movements. These devices often use mechanical rods [34], motor-controlled strings [35], or other physical mechanisms. The stimulation is sensed by the human kinesthetic system [36] as force feedback. Force feedback has a range of useful cases. For example, it can help visually impaired people understand visual content via an emulator. A haptic surface tablet can generate force feedback for visually impaired users. These users are given information about the tactile properties of a displayed image, aiding in the perception and comprehension of the content [37]. In virtual reality (VR), force feedback enhances the visual emulation of the physical world by simulating reaction forces when interacting or manipulating VR objects [38]. In healthcare, force feedback

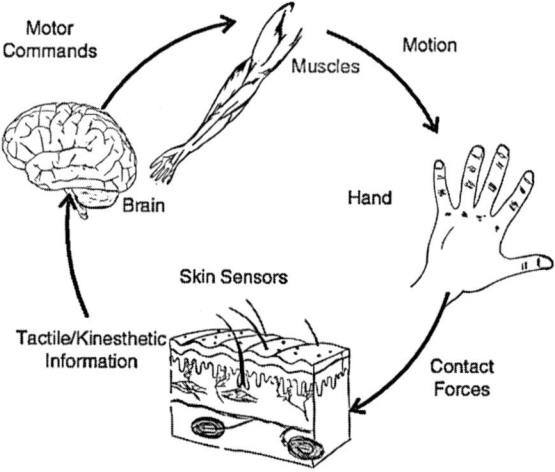

Fig. 1.1 Human Haptic System [33]. Upscaled, enhanced with freepik.ai

can enhance telesurgeries by providing surgeons with reaction forces on the picture at a distance [39], provided there is zero latency [40].

2. **Vibration:** Vibration of the skin is how humans identify the texture of surfaces, usually by sliding the fingers (that have microgroves). A human can't identify a surface without sliding its fingers over it. The human sense of touch processes vibration signal parameters such as frequency, amplitude, waveform, duration, and damping [41]. For example, a drummer uses all such information available to determine how strong the grip on the baton should be to achieve the desired damping characteristic of the hand-baton system. This is done via the human haptic system and relies less on the visual system, as the frequencies are often too fast, up to 200 BPM, and it is hard to estimate damping from the visual input. Vibrotactile devices have been leveraged in various applications to improve the user experience and performance in interactive tasks. These devices provide tactile information by applying pressure to the skin [36]. One use of vibrotactile devices is in VR, which can emulate collisions [42]. This feedback enhances the immersive experience and interaction with virtual environments. Even low-fidelity emulations are useful; the brain quickly learns to interpret them in minutes. In physical therapy and motor learning, vibrotactile feedback is used to help individuals learn new motor skills [43]. Evidence has shown that it reduces errors and improves the learning curve, particularly in arm motion training [43]. An alternative way to produce vibration is with ultrasounds. Ultrasonic phased arrays can create the effect of a surface mid-air (a.k.a a "metasurface"). These systems can also implement remote variable force feedback by tracking finger movements and focusing the ultrasound on the fingertips, improving user perception and control in mid-air interactive tasks [44].

3. **Thermal:** Such devices can create heat or cold sensations, improving realism [10]. This type of haptic technology has a wide range of potential applications. For instance, it can be integrated into assistive canes for visually challenged individuals, providing them with tactile feedback about the presence and location of obstacles [45]. Additionally, research is exploring the use of haptic technology for brain stimulation in patients with dementia or in a coma, potentially offering new avenues for treatment [20].

4. **Airflow:** Airflow feedback uses air jets to provide a nonintrusive interaction experience. This method allows for more freedom of movement and a greater sense of presence in virtual environments [46]. Researchers have developed pneumatic prototypes that simulate realistic air movements around the user, resulting in an overall enhanced and realistic VR experience [47].

5. **Electrical Nerve Stimulation:** Electrotactile systems harness electrodes and stimulators to gain tactile feedback by sending electrical currents through the skin and stimulating nerve endings. Electrotactile feedback directly affects the skin's subdermal area, bypassing skin receptors. This technology is used in many fields, including prosthetics, VR, robotics, and gaming [48]. For instance, [49] developed electrotactile feedback systems that use force sensors and transcutaneous electrical nerve stimulation (TENS) electrodes to enhance tactile sensations for amputees who use prosthetic hands.

6. **Electrical Muscle Stimulation:** Electrical muscle stimulation (EMS) is a technique that uses electrical impulses to induce muscle contractions directly. EMS has been used traditionally in rehabilitative medicine to regenerate lost motor functions [50]. EMS has also found novel applications in mobile contexts, transforming user interaction with digital experiences. From subtle muscle vibrations guiding pedestrian navigation [51] to force feedback in handheld games that tilts the device based on gameplay [52], EMS offers immersive possibilities. Even fitness activities like jogging can be enhanced with EMS-generated feedback mimicking real-world sensations like resistance or impact [53]. Sports training can similarly benefit, as EMS feedback during an interaction with a ball or object creates a more realistic experience [54].

Another way to classify haptics is by the user's action that caused the haptic sensation.

Then, haptics can be touchable, graspable, and wearable. Let's explore the details:

1. **Wearable:** Wearable haptics integrate haptic devices into clothing or accessories, enabling users to receive continuous touch feedback on their body, often due to movement [55]. These wearable systems can include fingertip devices for immersive virtual environments, vests for sensory replacement, or bands that deliver tactile stimuli, expanding how users experience haptic feedback [56]. Wearable haptic systems have the potential for natural and private communication between users and their environment [57]. For instance, fingertip devices typically provide localized feedback to specific areas of the hand or fingers, enabling precise interaction with virtual objects. Glove-based systems include the entire hand, providing comprehensive tactile feedback and natural hand movements. Further, exoskeleton devices augment the user's hand movements with external mechanical structures, offering force feedback and support for tasks requiring physical manipulation [58]. One of the first use of haptics in a wearable were the so called radio pagers of the 1980s (see Chap. 5).

2. **Touchable:** Touchable haptic devices involve direct interaction with a surface or device that provides localized feedback, such as a touch screen offering tactile responses, without requiring the user to wear additional equipment [15]. These devices utilize vibrotactile, electrostatic, or ultrasonic technologies to create a direct touch sensation on the user's skin [59]. A haptic pen is an example of a touchable haptic device [60]. It offers tactile feedback for a stylus-based touchscreen. It enables a wide range of tactile sensations by combining a pressure-sensitive stylus with a solenoid, enhancing user interaction in modern computing systems.

3. **Graspable:** Graspable haptic devices allow users to experience virtual objects' stiffness, texture, and shape through grasping and manipulation. This experience enhances interactions in virtual or remote environments [4]. For instance, [61] discussed integrating graspable devices into a mobile robot system. This integration facilitated two-point contact kinesthetic interactions, allowing users full locomotion in expansive virtual environments. Furthermore, [62] introduced a

novel haptic grasper offering touch sensations in 3-DoF motions, resembling the characteristics of graspable devices.

1.4 Key Drivers in the Advancement of Haptic Systems

Research has identified several motivations for developing haptic systems, including improving the user experience, military operational needs, and human factors.

Improving the user experience has been a driving force in developing haptic feedback systems, especially in overcoming the constraints of classic motor-based actuators [63]. In gaming, a key driver to improving haptic systems is to allow players to truly feel the action and nuance, enhancing realism beyond visuals and sound [64]. For example, improved haptics in gaming could let you feel the rattle of a powerful shotgun and the soft crunch of footsteps in the snow, adding realism beyond sights and sounds. This realism translates to improved usability and control, as the added realism fosters a more intuitive gameplay experience [65]. Improving the user experience has also been a noticeable key driver in tablets and phones. The technology provides additional sensory information, making technology more immersive and improving the conveyance of non-verbal information [66].

Recent advances have focused on using active materials and actuation mechanisms for flexible, stretchable, and high-resolution haptic feedback to overcome these constraints. These improvements aim to deliver advanced touch sensitivities and improve the user experience effectively [67].

Military operational needs have also been crucial in advancing haptic systems [68]. These systems have shown their potential to improve performance through experiments conducted in various settings, including laboratory environments and real-world combat scenarios [69]. Military operators have effectively used vibrotactile signals in difficult contexts, such as combat vehicles, aircrew cockpits, fast-moving watercraft, underwater environments, and physically demanding exercises [70]. Furthermore, tactile warnings can enhance performance during tasks such as robot control and unmanned aerial vehicle (UAV) operations [71].

Furthermore, human factors have affected the development and deployment of haptic systems. Indeed, psychophysical advances have paved the way for haptic system innovations by emphasizing human sensory experiences, such as intensity, quality, extension, and duration [72]. Jones and Tan [72] examined psychophysical methodologies in haptic research, including methods for measuring absolute and difference thresholds as well as factors influencing participants' reactions. They emphasized the significance of knowing the factors that impact perceptual processing. Possible factors include the stimulus context, the range of stimuli presented, the sequence of stimulus presentation, and the spacing between stimuli.

1.5   Applications and Limitations of Haptic Systems

Haptic systems have applications in various fields. In healthcare, they function as assistive technology. For example, they can offer feedback for tasks such as navigation and object manipulation to aid individuals with disabilities [15]. Furthermore, haptic feedback can be useful in simulations. These simulations provide trainees with immersive experiences, allowing them to emulate real medical procedures. As such, haptics can help practitioners refine essential skills in invasive and interventional techniques within a controlled and safe virtual environment [73]. Other applications of haptics in healthcare include soft robotics and tactile sensing. These haptic technologies have been developed for medical diagnosis, prosthetics, neurorobotics, surgery, and physiotherapy. These technologies can also be used to provide personalized care to patients [74]. The use of haptics is also being explored in telemedicine. For example, [75] developed a system combining haptics, VR, and telemedicine to help patients achieve long-term healing. This system is intended to reduce transportation expenses, promote exercise, and decrease patient isolation.

Haptic feedback can enhance gaming and entertainment experiences by providing tactile sensations that improve immersion. It enables users to receive visual and auditory stimuli, combining them for a more immersive experience. Haptic feedback can also be used to evaluate user performance or as a substitute for vision or motor skills [76]. Haptic technology can make games more accessible for people with visual impairments. For example, a haptic device (HapTech) provides audio and haptic feedback to visually impaired users [77]. Designed to help users enjoy an enriched gaming experience, this device is portable, lightweight, and easily reprogrammable.

The entertainment industry can also use haptic technology to create immersive and interactive environments [78]. These enhanced VR experiences make the entertainment more realistic.

Haptic technology can be useful in space exploration. For example, haptic technology integrated into spacesuits can enhance astronaut performance and safety during extravehicular activities. For instance, haptic footwear can vibrate to alert the astronaut to their proximity to an antenna or an invisible rock while walking [79]. Haptics can also help us interact with and visualize data from distant planets, leading to improved planning and execution of space missions. For instance, Basdogen et al. (2002) developed a haptic system that allows users to touch and manipulate virtual objects in a stereo-vision environment without needing special eyewear. Additionally, haptic teleoperation can help control robots designed for space exploration missions. By controlling robots, operators can manipulate the robot's position and orientation with enhanced immersion and feedback. Liu et al. [80] designed two specialized haptic joysticks and implemented a hybrid motion mapping method with a haptic feedback model. These controllers provide a sense of touch, letting operators "feel" the remote environment. The key lies in a hybrid mapping method that adapts control for both precision and maneuverability, along with haptic feedback that simulates the resistance the remote machine encounters. This allows operators to better interact with distant robots and probes.

The success of haptic systems in various applications does not come without challenges. These challenges include the high cost and size of devices, limited workspace, and inadequate force feedback [81]. In healthcare, the lack of haptic feedback in surgical robotics can affect the surgeon's ability to feel what they interact with [82]. This issue can impact the precision and safety of robot-assisted procedures. Similarly, haptic feedback in VR is rather poor compared to the abundant haptic properties that humans can perceive in the physical world [83]. Indeed, accurately reproducing the sense of touch remains a significant challenge [84].

1.6 Overview of the Book

This book explores haptic technology, its effect on different industries, the challenges it faces, and its potential for the future. The first chapter introduces haptic technology and devices. It examines the historical context of haptics and explains key drivers that led to advancements in tactile feedback systems. It also highlights the potential of haptic technology in various industries.

The second chapter explores how haptic technology is transforming the healthcare industry. It shows how haptic feedback is utilized in medical simulations, surgical training, and patient rehabilitation. This chapter highlights the impact of haptic technology and its potential to transform the medical industry.

The third chapter discusses the role of haptic technology in the gaming industry. It discusses how haptic feedback devices revolutionize the industry by creating interactive and realistic virtual environments. It focuses on haptics transforming VR and integrating haptic feedback and tactile sensations to innovate gameplay mechanics.

The fourth chapter examines the challenges of using haptics in real-world applications. It discusses technical complexities, ergonomic considerations, and compatibility issues in applying haptics in different domains. The chapter also addresses the ongoing research and development in creating effective haptic-based systems.

The fifth chapter discusses the future and trends of haptic technology and its usage in novel contexts. It reviews the adoption rates of haptics across various industries and provides insights into the latest patents on haptics for various applications, including healthcare, gaming, and automotive industries.

Finally, the sixth chapter summarizes the key takeaways from various use cases and applications of haptic technology. This chapter concludes by focusing on overcoming haptics' limitations and the exciting possibilities of this emerging technology.

1.7   Conclusion

In summary, haptic technology has significantly revolutionized multiple industries, enhancing user experiences by providing more intuitive and increasingly immersive interactions. In healthcare, haptic feedback enhances surgical precision and training through simulators that provide tactile responses. In the gaming and entertainment industry, haptic technology elevates user immersion by replicating the tactile sensations of virtual environments, making experiences more engaging and realistic. Haptics can also be used in novel contexts, such as space exploration, to improve astronaut safety. Haptic technology has its roots in the physiological study of touch and extends into innovative technological applications. Haptic systems can be categorized based on their interaction style (wearable, touchable, graspable) and the type of feedback they provide (force, tactile, thermal, airflow).

Acknowledgements This research was funded by the joint UAEU-ZU grant no. R22021.

References

1. Kapoor, S., et al.: Haptics: touchfeedback technology widening the horizon of medicine. J. Clin. Diagn. Res. JCDR **8**(3), 294–299 (2014)
2. Lederman, S.J., Klatzky, R.L.: Haptic perception: A tutorial. Atten. Percept. Psychophys. **71**(7), 1439–1459 (2009). https://doi.org/10.3758/APP.71.7.1439
3. Sagaya Aurelia, P.: Haptics: prominence and challenges. In: Hemanth, D. (ed.) Human Behaviour Analysis Using Intelligent Systems, pp. 21–43. Springer (2019)
4. Sreelakshmi, M., Subash, T.: Haptic technology: a comprehensive review on its applications and future prospects. Mater. Today Proceed. **4**, 4182–4187 (2017)
5. Chun, S., et al.: An artificial neural tactile sensing system. Nat. Electr. **4**, 429–438 (2021)
6. Novich, S., Eagleman, D.: Using space and time to encode vibrotactile information: toward an estimate of the skin's achievable throughput. Exp. Brain Res. **233**, 2777–2788 (2015)
7. Uysal, S.: The spinal cord. In: Uysal, S. (ed.) Functional Neuroanatomy and Clinical Neuroscience: Foundations for Understanding Disorders of Cognition and Behavior Get access Arrow, p. 75. Oxford University Press, Oxford (2023)
8. Hultborn, H.: Spinal reflexes, mechanisms and concepts: from Eccles to Lundberg and beyond. Prog. Neurobiol. **78**(3–5), 215–232 (2006)
9. Lindeman, R., Page, R., Yanagida, Y., Sibert, J.: Towards Full-Body Haptic Feedback: The Design and Deployment of a Spatialized Vibrotactile Feedback System. In: Proceedings of the ACM Symposium on Virtual Reality Software and Technology, New York (2004)
10. Giri, G., Maddahi, Y., Zareinia, K.: An application-based review of haptics technology **10**(1) (2021)
11. Kim, E., Schneider, O.: Defining Haptic Experience: Foundations for Understanding, Communicating, and Evaluating CHI 2020, Honolulu, HI (2020)
12. Bau, O., Poupyrev, I., Israr, A., Harrison, C.: TeslaTouch: electrovibration for touch surfaces. In: Proceedings of the 23nd Annual ACM Symposium on User Interface Software And Technology—UIST '10, New York (2010)
13. Winfield, L., Glassmire, J., Colgate, J.E., Peshkin, M.: T-PaD: tactile pattern display through variable friction reduction. In: Second Joint EuroHaptics Conference and Symposium on Haptic Interfaces for Virtual Environment and Teleoperator Systems (WHC'07) (2007)

14. Carter, T., et al.: UltraHaptics: multi-point mid-air haptic feedback for touch surfaces. In: Proceedings of the 26th Annual ACM Symposium on User Interface Software and Technology (UIST '13). Andrews Scotland (2013)
15. Kern, T., Hatzfeld, C., Abbasimoshaei, A.: Engineering Haptic Devices. Springer (2023)
16. Brewster, S., Chohan, F., Brown, L.: Tactile feedback for mobile interactions. San Jose California USA. In: Proceedings of the SIGCHI Conference on Human Factors in Computing Systems (CHI'07) (2007)
17. Massie, T.H., Salisbury, J.K.: The PHANTOM haptic interface: a device for probing virtual objects. In: Proceedings of the ASME Winter Annual Meeting, Symposium on Haptic Interfaces for Virtual Environment (1994)
18. Lacote, I., et al.: 'Tap Stimulation': An Alternative To Vibrations To Convey The Apparent Haptic Motion Illusion. Virtual, IEEE Haptics Symposium, HAPTICS (2022)
19. Park, G., et al.: Tactile effect design and evaluation for virtual buttons on a mobile device touchscreen. In: Proceedings of the 13th International Conference on Human Computer Interaction with Mobile Devices and Services (MobileHCI '11) (2011)
20. Gabriel, J., Silva, A., Restivo, M., Pinheiro, I.: Brain Stimulation Using an Haptic Thermal Device. In: Experiment@ International Conference (exp.at'13) Coimbra (2013)
21. Singhal, Y., Wang, H., Gil, H., Kim, J.: Mid-air thermo-tactile feedback using ultrasound haptic display. In: Proceedings of the 27th ACM Symposium on Virtual Reality Software and Technology (2021)
22. Morgan, M.: Review: the sense of touch. Perception **8**(6), 78–235 (1979)
23. Jütte, R.: Haptic perception: an historical approach. In: Grunwald, M. (ed.) Human Haptic Perception: Basics and Applications, pp. 3–13 (2008)
24. Brooks, S., Frederick, P., Fuchs, P.: Advanced Technology for Portable Personal Visualization. AD-A261 (1993)
25. Chang, A., et al.: ComTouch: Design of a Vibrotactile Communication Device. Association for Computing Machinery (2002)
26. Minsky, M., et al.: Feeling and seeing: issues in force display. SIGGRAPH Comput. Graph. **24**(4), 235–241 (1990)
27. Buttolo, P., Hannaford, B.: Pen-based force display for precision manipulation in virtual environments. In: Proceedings Virtual Reality Annual International Symposium '95. Research Triangle Park, NC (1995)
28. Iwata, H.: History of haptic interface. In: Grunwald, M. (ed.) Human Haptic Perception: Basics and Applications, pp. 355–361. Birkhäuser Basel (2008)
29. Goertz, R.C.: Anti-Swing Crane with Anti-Creep Variable Speed Hoisting, 1st edn. University of Michigan Library, Ann Arbor (1952)
30. Ohnishi, K., Mizoguchi, T.: Real haptics and its applications. IEEJ Trans. Electr. Electr. Eng. **12**(6), 803–808 (2017)
31. See, A., Choco, J., Chandramohan, K.: Touch, texture and haptic feedback: a review on how we feel the world around US. Appl. Sci. **12**, 4686 (2022)
32. Wang, D., Ohnishi, K., Xu, W.: Multimodal haptic display for virtual reality: a survey. IEEE Trans. Ind. Electr. **67**(1), 617–623 (2020)
33. Saddik, A., Orozco, M., Eid, M., Cha, J.: Human haptic perception. In: Haptics Technologies: Bringing Touch to Multimedia. Springer (2011)
34. Mellis, D. A., Banzi, M., Cautielles, D., Igoe, T.: Arduino: An Open Electronics Prototyping Platform. CHI '07 Extended Abstracts, San Jose (2007)
35. Hirata, Y., Sato, M.: 3-dimensional interface device for virtual work space. IEEE/RSJ Int. Confer. Intell. Robots Syst. (1992)
36. Oakley, I., McGee, M., Brewster, S., Gray, P.: Putting the feel in 'look and feel'. In: Conference on Human Factors in Computing Systems (2000)
37. Gay, S., Rivière, M., Pissaloux, E.: Towards haptic surface devices with force feedback for visually impaired people. In: International Conference on Computers Helping People with Special Needs, Linz (2018)

38. Antonya, C.: Force feedback in string based haptic systems. Proced. Comput. Sci. **25**, 90–97 (2012)
39. Patel, R., Atashzar, S., Tavakoli, M.: Haptic feedback and force-based teleoperation in surgical robotics. Proceed. IEEE **110**, 1012–1027 (2022)
40. Chatterjee, S.D.M.: Advancements in Robotic Surgery: Innovations, Challenges, and Future Prospects (2024). https://doi.org/10.1007/s11701-023-01801-w
41. Alahakone, A., Senanayake, S.: Vibrotactile Feedback Systems: Current Trends in Rehabilitation, Sports and Information Display, pp. 1148–1153. Singapore (2009)
42. Schätzle, S., Ende, T., Wüsthoff, T., Preusche, C.: VibroTac: an ergonomic and versatile usable vibrotactile feedback device. In: Proceedings of the 19th International Symposium in Robot and Human Interactive Communication (2010)
43. Bark, K., et al.: Effects of vibrotactile feedback on human learning of arm motions. IEEE Trans. Neural Syst. Rehabil. Eng. **23**, 51–63 (2014)
44. Liu, Y., et al.: Construction of ultrasonic tactile force feedback model in teleoperation robot system. Sensors **21**(7), 548 (2021)
45. Kim, S., et al.: Two-dimensional thermal haptic module based on a flexible thermoelectric device. Soft Robot **7**(6), 736–742 (2020)
46. Tsalamlal, M., Issartel, P., Ouarti, N., Ammi, M.: HAIR: HAptic feedback with a mobile AIR jet. IEEE **12**, 2699–2706 (2014)
47. Rietzler, M., et al.: VaiR: simulating 3D airflows in virtual reality. In: Proceedings of the 2017 CHI Conference on Human Factors in Computing Systems (2017)
48. Kourtesis, P., et al.: Electrotactile feedback applications for hand and arm interactions: a systematic review, meta-analysis, and future directions. IEEE Trans. Haptics **15**(3), 479–496 (2022)
49. Pamungkas, D., Ward, K.: Electro-Tactile Feedback System for a Prosthetic Hand, pp. 1–12 (2015)
50. Lopes, P., Baudisch, P.: Interactive systems based on electrical muscle stimulation. Computer **50**(10), 28–35 (2017)
51. Pfeiffer, M., et al.: Cruise control for pedestrians: controlling walking direction using electrical muscle stimulation. In: Proceedings of the 33rd Annual ACM Conference on Human Factors in Computing Systems, CHI '15 (2015)
52. Lopes, P., Baudisch, P.: Muscle-propelled force feedback: bringing force feedback to mobile devices. In: CHI '13: Proceedings of the SIGCHI Conference on Human Factors in Computing Systems, Paris (2013)
53. Hassan, M., et al.: FootStriker: an EMS-based foot strike assistant for running. Proceed. ACM Interact. Mobile Wear. Ubiquit. Technol. **1**(1), 1–18 (2017)
54. Farbiz, F., Yu, Z.H., Manders, C., Ahmad, W.: An Electrical Muscle Stimulation Haptic Feedback for Mixed Reality Tennis Game. ACM SIGGRAPH 2007 posters, San Diego, CA (2007)
55. Kajimoto, H.: Wearable haptics. J. Instit. Electr. Eng. Jpn. **141**(2), 71–73 (2021)
56. Pacchierotti, C., et al.: Wearable haptic systems for the fingertip and the hand: taxonomy, review, and perspectives. IEEE Trans. Haptics **10**, 580–600 (2017)
57. He, S., Jing, Y., Lu, Y., Liu, Z.: Wearable Haptic Interfaces and Systems (2023)
58. Van Wegen, M., et al.: An overview of wearable haptic technologies and their performance in virtual object exploration. Sensors **23**(3), 1563 (2023)
59. Adilkhanov, A., Rubagotti, M., Kappassov, Z.: Haptic devices: wearability-based taxonomy and literature review. IEEE Access **10**, 91923–91947 (2022)
60. Lee, J., et al.: Haptic Pen: A Tactile Feedback Stylus for Touch Screens, pp. 291–294 (2004)
61. Pascale, M., Formaglio, A., Prattichizzo, D.: A mobile platform for haptic grasping in large environments. Virtual Reality **12**, 11–23 (2006)
62. Pediredla, V., Chandrasekaran, K., Annamraju, S., Asokan, T.: Design and realization of a novel haptic graspable interface for augmenting touch sensations. Front. Robot. AI (2022)
63. Pezent, E., et al.: Explorations of wrist haptic feedback for AR/VR interactions with tasbi. In: Extended Abstracts of the 2020 CHI Conference on Human Factors in Computing Systems (CHI EA '20) (2020)

64. Kim, H.-Y., Kim, J.: A study of implementation of kinesthetic feedback on game framework using the haptic device for realistic interaction. Int. J. Appl. Eng. Res. **10**(10), 27205–27212 (2015)
65. Han, P.-H., et al.: BoEs: attachable haptics bits on gaming controller for designing interactive gameplay. In: SIGGRAPH Asia 2017 VR Showcase (SA '17), Bangkok (2017)
66. Mandeville, A., Birnbaum, D., Sampanes, C.: Remote Touch: Humanizing Social Interactions in Technology Through Multimodal Interfaces. In: Proceedings of the 9th International Conference, VAMR (2017)
67. Yang, T., et al.: Recent advances and opportunities of active materials for haptic technologies in virtual and augmented reality. Adv. Funct. Mater. **31**(39), 456 (2021)
68. van Erp, J., Self, B.: Introduction to tactile displays in military environments. In: Tactile Displays for Orientation, Navigation and Communication in Air, Sea, pp. 1–13. Research and Technology Organisation (2008)
69. Brill, J., Terrence, P., Stafford, S., Gilson, R.: A wireless tactile communication system for conveying U.S. army hand-arm signals. Proceed. Hum. Fact. Ergon. Soc. Annu. Meet. **50**(20), 32–65 (2006)
70. Salzer, Y., Oron-Gilad, T., Ronen, A., Parmet, Y.: Vibrotactile "on-thigh" alerting system in the cockpit. Hum. Factors J. Hum. Fact. Ergon. Soc. **53**, 118–131 (2011)
71. Elliott, L., Schmeisser, E., Redden, E.: Development of tactile and haptic systems for U.S. infantry navigation and communication. In: Smith, M.S.G. (ed.) Human Interface and the Management of Information. Interacting with Information. Human Interface, pp. 399–407 (2011)
72. Jones, L., Tan, H.: Application of psychophysical techniques to haptic research. IEEE Trans. Haptics **6**, 268–284 (2013)
73. Wei, L.Z., et al.: Haptics-driven healthcare training simulator systems. In: Nestel, D., Kelly, B.J.M., Watson, M. (eds.) Healthcare Simulation Education: Evidence, Theory and Practice (2017)
74. Anon: Advancing Soft, Tactile, and Haptic Technologies: Recent Developments for Healthcare Applications (2024)
75. Broeren, J., Dixon, M., Sunnerhagen, K., Rydmark, M.: Rehabilitation After Stroke Using Virtual Reality, Haptics (Force Feedback) and Telemedicine. National Library of Medicine (2006)
76. Deng, S., Chang, J., Zhang, J.: A survey of haptics in serious gaming. Lect. Notes Comput. Sci. **42**, 8605 (2014)
77. Walia, A., Goel, P., Kairon, V., Jain, M.: HapTech: Exploring Haptics in Gaming for the Visually Impaired, pp. 1–6 (2020)
78. Saint-Louis, C., Hamam, A.: Survey of haptic technology and entertainment applications. In: SoutheastCon 2021, pp. 1–7 (2021)
79. Kuhail, M., et al.: Haptic systems: trends and lessons learned for haptics in spacesuits. Electronics **12**(8), 54002 (2023)
80. Liu, G., Geng, X., Liu, L., Wang, Y.: Haptic based teleoperation with master-slave motion mapping and haptic rendering for space exploration. Chin. J. Aeronaut. **32**(3), 723–736 (2019)
81. Saddik, A.: The potential of haptics technologies. IEEE Instrum. Measur. Mag. **10**, 10–17 (2007)
82. Enayati, N., Momi, E., Ferrigno, G.: Haptics in robot-assisted surgery: challenges and benefits. IEEE Rev. Biomed. Eng. **9**, 49–65 (2016)
83. Wang, D., et al.: Haptic display for virtual reality: progress and challenges. Virtual Reality Intell. Hardware **1**(2), 136–162 (2019)
84. Van Den Berg, D., et al.: Challenges in haptic communications over the tactile internet. IEEE Access **54**, 23502–23518 (2017)

Chapter 2
Exploring the Role of Haptic Technology in Healthcare

Abstract Using haptic technology has advanced outcomes in various areas of healthcare, such as telemedicine, rehabilitation, and surgical training. It has also furthered the use cases of medical devices in the form of wearables such as gloves and smart insoles, among others. This chapter examines the current state of haptics in healthcare by reviewing how haptic technology is employed and highlighting novel applications. Specifically, our review focuses on the areas of surgery simulation, gait support, and fitness tracking. In terms of medical outcomes, our findings show that using vibration and force-based haptics is correlated with improved treatment outcomes as well as with more effective medical training.

Keywords Haptics · Healthcare · Telemedicine · Training

2.1 Introduction

Physicians have historically relied heavily on touch to examine patients [1]. With technological advancements such as haptic miniaturization [2], and the commoditization of wearable devices [3], it is now possible to provide medical devices and solutions that incorporate haptic technology at reasonable costs to both patients and practitioners [4].

In general, incorporating haptics in medical solutions improves the comprehensiveness and effectiveness of outcomes in medical treatments. For example, haptics has been incorporated into a range of applications such as telemedicine, rehabilitation, surgical training, and beyond [5]. Haptics in wearables, such as gloves and smart insoles, are increasingly used in healthcare, highlighting the added utility [6]. On the educational side, haptic simulators have also been introduced in medical curricula (e.g., Ohio University curriculum) due to their improvement of training programs of clinical skills [7]. Indeed, haptics seems to easily integrate and complement traditional training approaches that do not use haptics. Studies have shown that incorporating feedback into virtual reality (VR) telemedicine consultations improves clinical outcomes. The study found that VR training with haptic feedback significantly improved initial performance during the use of a surgical drill, leading to higher confidence and a more realistic simulation [8]. Specifically, haptics can provide more realistic training conditions, such as recreating how tissue density is sensed during a procedure [9]. Apart from more realistic surgery simulations, it positively impacts inclusivity. For example, using haptics can ease the accessibility of individuals with disabilities by simply enhancing the control of smart prostheses, among other use cases [10]. These and other practical applications have demonstrated haptics' positive and multifaceted impact on healthcare [4].

This chapter provides an in-depth exploration of how haptics is used in healthcare. The goal is to offer the reader an overview of the different types of haptic technologies employed and the unique challenges they address. To accomplish this, we review and examine various technologies we deem key in healthcare applications. These are force-based haptics, vibration-based haptics, electrical muscle stimulation (EMS), and transcutaneous electrical nerve stimulation (TENS) when used to bypass touch receptors.

The chapter is structured as follows: First, it covers applications of haptics in healthcare (Sect. 2.2). Then, it presents the types of haptics used in healthcare (Sect. 2.3) and explains the technology's context of use (Sect. 2.4). Finally, the chapter concludes with the main findings (Sect. 2.5).

2.2 Applications of Haptics in Healthcare

Table 2.1 shows an overview of current applications of haptics in healthcare. According to [11], integrating artificial intelligence (AI), immersive technologies [e.g., VR and augmented reality (AR)], and haptics into medical imaging devices elevates telemedicine outcomes by enabling medical practitioners to experience the sensation of touch while performing surgical operations remotely. On the other hand, [12] explored using haptic gloves in telerehabilitation. These gloves provide tactile feedback and resistance, simulating the touch and feel of physical therapy exercises. They are particularly beneficial for remote rehabilitation, allowing patients to receive guided physical therapy from their homes while ensuring that movements are performed correctly.

Haptics has also been used to assist in medical training and surgery simulations. For example, CyberGlove systems have been used in medical training because they can capture the 3D motion of the hand, offering tactile feedback with vibrotactile actuators on each finger and palm [13].

Immersive technologies combined with haptics have been used in medical training. COVID-19 social distancing restrictions have significantly impacted the advancement of haptic technology, as physical training has been replaced with virtual training through VR and AR technologies to simulate operations [14]. Virtual training has been improved by VR and AR applications that simulate object grasping of various grip forces and weights. These applications improve user interaction and

Table 2.1 An overview of some of the applications of haptics in healthcare

Application	Haptic device and references
Telemedicine and telerehabilitation	• AR/VR head-mounted device (HMD) [11] • Haptic gloves [12]
Medical training and surgery simulation	• CyberGlove [13] • VR headsets, haptic suits [14] • Grabity, LinkTouch [15] • Ring, TacTiles, LucidVR, ExoTen [16] • Haptic simulators for dental training [17] • Vision-haptic device integrated dental training simulation System [18] • Haptic similar for brain surgery training [19] • Maxillofacial surgical simulator [18] • Amputation simulator with bone sawing haptic interaction [20] • A haptic device for knee bone drilling in a serious game [21] • VR simulator of high tibial osteotomy for medical training [22]
Gait analysis and support	• Shoe Insole [23–26] • Sandals [27]
Rehabilitation	• Smart Shoe (VR) [28] • Shoe Insole + vibrotactile belt [29] • Stimulator device [4, 30] • E-textile gloves [31] • Haptic interfaces [32]
Voice therapy	• Dualpex 961 [33]
Sports performance enhancement	• Enraf Nonius S82 model [34]
Navigation, fitness tracking	• Shoe Insole [35]
Exercise error detection and correction	• Teslasuit [36]
Automatic improper loading posture detection and correction	• Metawear MMR wireless sensors [37]
Hearing impairment	• Sensory Augmentation [38]
Motor relearning after stroke	• Haptic therapy devices [39]

perception by providing tactile feedback and vibrotactile sensations for high stiffness and weight force feedback. In addition, wearable haptic devices such as LinkTouch pinpoint force sensation at the fingertip [15]. These significant advancements in VR technology led to authentic tactile experiences. For example, hRing is a haptic device that offers tactile feedback by stretching the skin on the finger, emulating the sensation of touch or grip. TacTiles are another wearable haptic device that generates an extra feeling of pressure on the skin by using tactile immersion in VR. LucidVR is also a wearable haptic device that allows direct engagement with virtual objects in a VR environment. Lastly, ExoTen is a haptic wearable device that simulates VR muscle contractions and movements [16].

Haptics have also been used in various types of surgeries. For example, a study on dental surgery simulation [17] introduced a haptic simulator designed for dental training. The simulator allows dental students to practice various procedures, providing tactile feedback mimicking the sensation of working on real teeth and gums. This haptic feedback is crucial for developing fine motor skills and a realistic sense of touch, each an essential in dental surgery.

Haptics have also been used in brain surgery haptic simulation [19]. This research identified the mechanical properties of brain parenchyma to create a realistic haptic simulation for brain surgery training. By simulating the tactile feel of brain tissue, the simulator helps neurosurgeons practice delicate brain surgery techniques in a controlled, risk-free environment, enhancing their skills and precision. Moreover, a maxillofacial surgical simulation study [18] offered haptic feedback for maxillofacial surgery training. It simulates the touch and resistance encountered during facial bone surgeries, helping surgeons develop a tactile understanding of different facial structures. This approach improves surgical accuracy and reduces potential risks in actual surgeries. Another example of surgery is amputation simulation [20]. The amputation simulator described in this study provides a haptic experience with bone sawing. This simulation is crucial for training surgeons in the tactile aspects of amputation, including the feeling of cutting through different tissue types and bones. It aids in preparing surgeons for the physical and technical challenges of amputations.

There are several applications of haptics in knee surgery. For example, a study on knee bone drilling [21] utilized two low-end haptic devices (Novint Falcon and Geomagic 3D Touch) for simulating knee bone drilling, typically used in orthopedic surgeries. Haptic feedback allows medical students to experience the resistance and sensation of drilling into bone, enhancing their understanding and skills in orthopedic procedures. Moreover, haptics has also been used in high tibial osteotomy simulations [22]. This VR simulation incorporates haptic feedback for high tibial osteotomy training. The haptic element provides realistic sensations of cutting and manipulating bone, which is crucial for orthopedic surgeons to understand the tactile nuances of this specific surgical procedure.

Haptic systems have been utilized in gait correction and analysis. Berengueres et al. [23] designed a smart insole to correct the condition of fallen arches in the foot. When the insole detects fallen arches, it nudges the user. Other smart insoles have targeted the knee, hips, and back as part of foot posture correction.

In addition, posture correction devices have been developed with other purposes in mind. For example, Niroshan [24] developed a shoe insole that can be inserted into shoes to provide comfort and support through vibration feedback. These vibrations help elderly individuals monitor and manage their balance while walking and standing and provide preventative help for diabetic users experiencing foot ulcers through low-level light therapy [25] focused on elderly individuals at risk of falling due to gait disorders or physical decline. These shoe insoles utilize vibrotactile feedback to assist with gait and balance.

Another application area is enhancing prostheses, such as lower limb prostheses, during stair descent. In this particular use case, a tailored shoe insole equipped with four force sensors collects data. The data is then processed and sent to vibrotactile actuators to provide feedback that improves proprioception [26]. Another area of application is helping patients with cognitive impairments. An example is the Sole-Sound system. The system is designed to adjust how wearers perceive the ground while walking using audio and haptic feedback integrated into the sandals. This fusion of sensory feedback positively influences the walking patterns of patients who have gait disorders from medical conditions such as Parkinson's disease [27]. Wang and Minor [28] used a robotic smart shoe for haptic terrain rendering in VR applications. The terrain rendering enhances walking experiences in gait training by adjusting the sole pressure and height in real time.

Rehabilitation is also a use case. Cesini et al. [29] designed a shoe insole with sensors paired with a vibrotactile belt. The insole was introduced as a rehabilitation tool for individuals with gait disorders. This system detects foot placement in real time. It provides immediate tactile feedback through a sensorized insole wirelessly connected to a textile waist belt equipped with vibrating motors, aiding in safer walking and reducing cognitive load. The combined use of the insole and belt shows high potential for enhancing rehabilitation, especially when the patient faces challenging terrains such as stairs. A study that used haptic interfaces [32] discussed using haptic interfaces in virtual rehabilitation as well. These interfaces provide realistic tactile sensations that mimic real-world interactions, which are suitably effective for virtual therapy sessions. They are particularly useful in scenarios where physical therapy needs to be more engaging or immersive, helping patients improve motor skills and coordination. Other rehabilitation applications include the treatment of sensory loss. This issue is a primary difficulty for patients with limb amputations. To address this limitation, patients used a simulation device to restore tactile sensations [30]. Stimulator devices with haptic technology have helped patients regain tactile perception, enhancing the recovery process in cases of postsurgery or trauma [4]. Novel forms of haptics have also been used in rehabilitation. Chan and Torah [31] introduced e-textile haptic feedback gloves equipped with a TENS unit to enhance tactile sensations in VR/AR environments. Integrating these gloves with a stimulator device offers a realistic touch experience for several rehabilitation scenarios.

Beyond applying haptics to well-known areas such as medical training, surgery simulation, assistance with gait, and rehabilitation, haptics is also applied to less popular areas. A few of these are voice therapy, sports performance enhancement, fitness and exercise, hearing impairment assistance, and motor relearning rehabilitation. For example, dysphonic patients use the TENS Dualpex 961 device. TENS helps the user to relax the cervical and perilaryngeal muscles, directly enhancing voice quality. Thus, TENS significantly improves affected individuals' voice therapy, function, and overall quality [33]. The performance of sports athletes can also be enhanced by using TENS. A study by César Colmenero utilized the Enraf Nonius S82 model to apply TENS to the quadriceps and hamstrings of athletes. It has also been effective in boosting athlete performance and reducing fatigue [34].

Lechal is a shoe insole that provides haptic navigation and precise fitness tracking (Fig. 2.1). The insole is embedded with advanced sensors that provide vibrations for direction and eliminate the need for constant phone checks. In addition, it monitors fitness metrics such as steps and calories [35]. Teslasuits play an important role

Fig. 2.1 Lechal shoe insoles
[35]

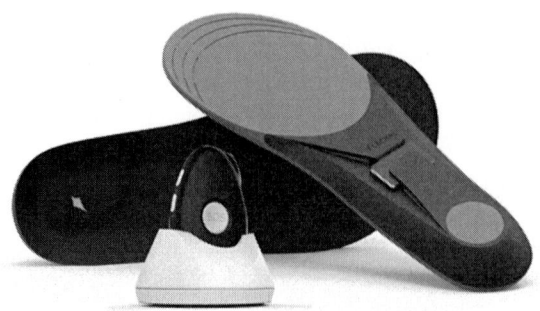

in virtual training by enhancing precision and reducing the mental strain of self-monitoring. A Teslasuit provides users with full-body haptic motion capture. The suit detects and immediately corrects exercise execution errors through real-time haptic feedback to ensure that users maintain accurate forms, thus improving fitness and reducing the possibility of injury [36].

Along with movements, haptics can help with posture and muscle loading. Kattoju et al. [37] used Metawear MMR wireless sensors to monitor and detect improper loading postures in real time. The system uses EMS to provide immediate feedback to the user to fix their posture if an improper loading posture is detected.

Furthermore, individuals with hearing impairments benefit from sensing environmental information in their surroundings to ensure safe interactions through sensory augmentation devices and tactile stimuli. For example, a specialized waterproof haptic device lets water polo athletes select the referee's whistle via vibrations [38]. Profita [40] presented a haptic device that helps individuals with hearing problems using Smart Garments equipped with sensors and actuators. These garments provide vibrotactile cues on the skin, which approximate the direction of important environmental sounds. This allows individuals with hearing impairments to receive contextual information about their surroundings, enhancing their ability to process ambient information and reducing exposure to potentially harmful situations.

Another application of haptics in healthcare is motor relearning after stroke. Ivanova et al. [39] focused on haptic therapy devices for motor relearning in stroke survivors. These devices provide sensory feedback to assist patients in relearning motor skills by guiding and correcting their movements. This tactile input is critical for retraining the brain and muscles to recover motor functions lost due to stroke.

2.3   Types of Haptics Used in Healthcare

Table 2.2 shows an overview of systems based on stimulating the sense of touch. Giri et al. [15] presented haptic devices that utilize EMS to enhance rehabilitation by directly training and stimulating the muscles. This feedback method offers direct muscle activation and helps patients enhance their recovery process and improve

Table 2.2 A partial overview of the haptic technologies by stimulation types in healthcare applications

Stimulation type	References
EMS	[15, 41]
IMU sensors and EMS	[37]
TENS	[30, 31, 33, 34, 36]
Vibration	[4, 13, 23–27, 29, 35, 38]
Force	[28, 42]
Vibration and force	[14, 43]

muscle function. Kattoju et al. [37] combined EMS and inertial measurement unit (IMU) sensors to accurately monitor and detect improper loading postures in real time by offering immediate posture correction.

TENS can augment patient senses in a variety of ways. Collu et al. [30] utilized TENS to restore sensory feedback in patients with limb amputation. This non-surgical approach has TENS trigger sensations in prosthetic systems, enhancing usability by sending electrical signals to the skin. Moreover, [31] employed TENS as a feedback method in e-textile gloves designed for VR/AR interactions. This technique provides electrotactile feedback, offering a tingling sensation to enhance user engagement in virtual environments. Integrating TENS in e-textile gloves ensures that the gloves remain flexible and breathable, improving user comfort and interaction in VR/AR applications. TENS can also provide muscle relaxation. Plotas et al. [33] described the effectiveness of TENS in voice therapy by relaxing the cervical and perilaryngeal muscles for patients suffering from dysphonia. This relaxation improves their voice quality. In another study, [34] utilized TENS to aid in recovering oral functions after orthognathic surgery. This intervention significantly improved the jaw opening and reduced inflammation post-surgery, thereby accelerating the recovery process for patients looking to restore their jaw's form and function.

TENS is also useful in providing real-time feedback. A Teslasuit utilizes TENS to correct exercise execution errors by detecting them through its sensors. This error detection ensures safer and more effective physical training, minimizing the risk of potential injuries. TENS shows promise in physical training and rehabilitation, offering immediate corrections and enhancing the overall quality of exercise execution [36].

Vibrotactile haptics have been used in various settings. For example, CyberGlove is a wearable device used for rehabilitation and training. CyberGlove is a valuable tool in healthcare for improving the assessment of hand function during rehabilitation. A recent study integrated CyberGlove and force-sensing resistors to measure finger joint flexion angles and fingertip forces during the Action Research Arm Test (ARAT). The haptics in CyberGlove provide real-time data on finger movements and forces, aiding in more accurate and quantitative evaluations. This enhanced assessment can lead to better rehabilitation outcomes by allowing therapists to tailor treatments more precisely to individual patient needs [44].

Vibrotactile haptics are also commonly used in footwear. For example, Lechal Footwear employs a haptic system using vibrotactile haptics to offer users intuitive navigation and fitness tracking. This system provides feedback that guides users through vibrations, providing detailed route guidance to ensure they stay on the right path. This route guidance particularly benefits individuals with visual impairment, helping them navigate their way and encouraging physical activity through accurate fitness metrics [35]. Another example of a vibrotactile haptic application is the Vibrasole shoe insole. This insole employs tactile, haptic feedback to enhance balance and gait in elderly individuals with diabetes [24]. Using shoe insoles with vibrotactile feedback can also benefit patients with lower limb prostheses. This feedback provides foot placement and movement guidance, particularly during stair descent, helping users avoid the risk of missteps and falls. This technology promotes awareness and confidence in the mobility of prosthesis users [26]. Similarly, the SoleSound system provides sandals with haptic feedback, utilizing vibrotactile actuators to enhance the user's walking experience across different terrains. This innovative solution aims to assist Parkinson's patients in gait rehabilitation and training [27]. Moreover, [23] introduced an interactive insole by employing a tactile, haptic approach and utilizing vibrotactile actuators to provide real-time feedback for patients to correct improper foot postures. For patients at risk of falling, [25] used an insole embedded with vibrotactile feedback, offering real-time prompts to older adults. This feedback reduces their chance of falling by enhancing awareness and adaptability to various ground conditions and surfaces on which they walk.

Vibrotactile feedback benefits individuals with sensory and lower limb sensory deficits, assisting with level and stair walking [29]. Further, vibrotactile feedback is crucial in creating a safe environment for medical students, enabling them to gain practical experience through VR [4]. According to Ramones and del-Rio-Guerra [38], vibrotactile feedback helps individuals with hearing impairments perceive and interpret sounds through vibrations on their skin, improving their overall quality of life by enhancing environmental awareness.

Beyond vibrotactile haptics, some studies have used kinesthetic haptics in healthcare. Wang and Minor [28] presented a smart shoe robotic footwear designed for haptic terrain rendering. The shoe features a kinesthetic haptic system to give users an augmented sense of virtual terrains as they move. This augmentation is achieved through mechanical actuators, specifically the passive modulation of bladder pressure and height in the shoe sole, to mimic various terrains. In healthcare, such design holds promise for rehabilitation, especially in VR scenarios, offering enhanced walking experiences and potential gait therapies for conditions such as Parkinson's disease. Moreover, [16] highlighted the significance of using kinesthetic haptic feedback to replicate human touch.

Interestingly, some studies have combined tactile and kinesthetic haptics. Motaharifar et al. [14] emphasized the role of vibrotactile and kinesthetic haptic systems powered by electromechanical (EM) actuators in medical training. Integrating these haptic systems provides a safe, efficient, and repeatable training experience.

2.4 Context of Use of Haptics in Healthcare

Table 2.3 summarizes various technology types and their context of use. Minopoulos et al. [11] utilized haptics within the tactile internet (TI). The Tactile Internet is an emerging paradigm in next-generation mobile networks, designed to enable real-time, high-reliability haptic communication and control between humans, machines, and objects over the Internet [45]. This technology has significantly progressed across telemedicine, medical imaging, surgery, and training. Integrating it with medical image visualization has enhanced the precision of robotic surgeries.

The impact of haptics is evident in the altered dynamics of medical professional interactions with virtual environments. Incorporating AI-based haptic feedback has given rise to immersive experiences in training simulations and surgical procedures. A notable example of such an immersive experience is the CyberGlove [13], a device designed to capture hand and finger motions to convert them into real-time data. The CyberGlove, equipped with small vibrotactile stimulators on each finger and palm, provides tactile feedback. This feedback is beneficial in surgical training and simulation, ultimately enhancing the overall training process and improving surgical outcomes.

Lechal [35] is a shoe equipped with vibrotactile haptic feedback for fitness and navigation. This innovative shoe goes beyond step counting, incorporating distance measurement and calorie tracking features. In addition, the design includes hands-free navigation capabilities via vibration, allowing users to navigate without needing to check their devices.

Moreover, Niroshan [24] highlighted that this technology benefits older adults. Specifically, the shoe insole monitors and assists older adults in maintaining balance while walking or standing. The device aims to restore the lost sense of feeling in the foot by applying low random vibrations to the sole. This dual functionality improves walking and balance and addresses the broader objective of enhancing the overall sensory experience for elderly individuals.

Based on the insights of [26], a haptic system has been designed to instill a sense of safety and confidence to help individuals with lower limb prostheses, particularly during stair descent. This system improves the overall walking experience for prosthetic feet users by helping them comprehensively understand their foot positioning and movement.

Zantotto et al. [46] highlighted the role of simulating diverse ground surface interactions in enhancing the user's walking experience. This simulation modulates the user's perception of the ground surface, offering vibrotactile underfoot feedback. This feedback improves safety and stability, creating a core foundation for enhancing user experience and providing a more immersive walking sensation.

Vibrotactile feedback has proven to be a promising solution for patients dealing with overpronation, as highlighted by [23]. This technology offers the potential to address walking posture and stride issues. It can replace traditional orthotics, reducing discomfort and minimizing the risk of associated injuries. The result is a tangible improvement in gait, providing individuals with overpronation a more comfortable

Table 2.3 An overview of technology types and their context of use

Context of use	Technology type and references
Telemedicine, medical imaging, surgery, training	TI [11]
Surgical training and simulation	Vibrotactile [4, 13, 23–27, 29, 35]
Fitness tracking, hands-free, guiding the user via vibrations	
Enhancing balance and gait for elderly individuals; preventative measure for diabetic foot ulcers	
Assisting lower limb prosthesis users during stair descent for prosthetic foot	
The system provides underfoot feedback simulating different ground surface interactions, aiming to modulate the perception of the ground surface during walking	
Correcting overpronation in walking	
Differentiating types of soil, reducing risk of falling	
Assisting in ground-level walking and stair walking for lower-limb amputees	
Medical education, surgical intervention, medical examinations, and training; upper limb rehabilitation	
Medical training; teleoperation	Vibrotacticle and Kinaesthetic [14]
Tactile stimulation; surgical procedures	Vibrotacticle & Kinaesthetic [16]
Medical training; teleoperation	EMS [15, 37]
Restoring ideal lifting angles for torso inclination and knee bend during lifting activities	
Virtual reality locomotion interfaces for gait therapies, especially for disorders like Parkinson's and spinal cord injuries	Kinesthetic [28]
Restoring sensory feedback in amputees to enhance their interaction with prosthetic limbs	TENS [30, 31, 33, 34, 36, 38]
Sports, daily activities for hearing-impaired individuals	
Simulate tactile sensations of virtual objects	
Treatment for dysphonia, muscle relaxation, pain alleviation	
Postsurgical recovery of patients who have undergone orthognathic surgery	
Movement assessment during physical exercises	

and stable walking experience. The integration of haptic technology, specifically vibrotactile and kinesthetic feedback, plays a crucial role, as emphasized by [14]. This integration becomes particularly significant in advancing medical training and teleoperation.

Shoe insoles equipped with tactile, haptic feedback serve a crucial role for older individuals at a greater risk of falling, allowing them to differentiate between ground types [25]. This insole enables users to modify their gait by providing tactile feedback and an augmented sense of the ground. Beyond the aging population, individuals with lower-limb amputations find valuable support in haptic devices that assist them during ground-level and stair walking [29]. Tactile feedback enhances individuals' confidence and independence while navigating, contributing to a more secure and self-assured mobility experience.

Integrating tactile systems and VR has improved medical operations, education, training, and quality [4]. This advancement became even more pertinent during the COVID-19 pandemic. Kinesthetic haptics have demonstrated their efficacy in enhancing surgical procedures by improving precision and safety, effectively bridging the gap between virtual and physical interactions.

The evolution of medical training and teleoperation is marked by improvements in haptic technology, according to [15]. It emphasizes EMS, allowing medical students to gain precise and reliable training in virtual and augmented reality environments. Furthermore, as discussed by Kattoju [37], integrating IMU sensors and EMSs is used to detect and rectify improper loading postures, this functionality stimulates specific muscles, guiding users to adjust their posture—an essential aspect of comprehensive medical training and teleoperation.

Wang and Minor [28] introduced a soft robotic smart shoe employing kinesthetic haptic feedback and presented a promising solution for gait therapies to benefit patients with Parkinson's disease and spinal cord injuries. Collu et al. [30] highlighted TENS as a significant tool for evoking referred tactile sensations in patients with limb amputation. TENS achieves this by stimulating underlying nerves through external electrodes placed on the skin, creating a nuanced and sensory-rich experience for individuals. Advancements in haptic devices extend their reach to individuals with hearing impairment, enhancing their engagement in sports and daily activities [38]. Chan and Torah [31] introduced gloves designed to simulate the tactile sensations of virtual objects. These gloves utilize TENS to provide electrotactile feedback and integrate tangible sensations through e-textiles, presenting a multisensory experience for the user.

The therapeutic potential of TENS has further expanded into the domain of dysphonia and voice disorders [33]. Cacho et al. [34] explored TENS as a viable treatment for postsurgical recovery in patients following orthognathic surgery. TENS effectively improves jaw opening and reduces inflammation, which is attributed to the muscle relaxation achieved through the TENS procedure. These findings suggest that TENS is an effective therapeutic tool for enhancing oral function and reducing associated inflammation after surgery.

The Teslasuit, introduced by [36], integrates haptic technology in movement assessment during physical exercise. This full-body haptic motion capture suite detects exercise execution errors in real time and employs TENS to provide imme-diate haptic feedback. The Teslasuit guides users to correct their movements, demonstrating its utility in real-time assessment and improvement during physical activities.

2.5 Conclusion

Alongside many other technologies (e.g., AI, robotics, genomic), haptics has seen increased adoption in healthcare. In particular, we highlighted enhancing telemedicine, remote surgeries, telerehabilitation with tactile feedback for physical therapy exercises, and enhancing the realism of simulated training of dental, brain, maxillofacial, and amputation surgeries. In orthopedic surgery, haptic systems simulate the sensations of bone manipulation, while in gait support, smart insoles correct walking posture and assist with balance, especially for individuals with lower limb prostheses. In rehabilitation, haptic technology helps improve motor skills and coordination and supports limb amputees. Additionally, haptic systems are used in voice therapy, sports performance enhancement, fitness tracking, aiding those with hearing impairments, and facilitating motor relearning in stroke survivors.

Various technologies stimulating the sense of touch have been used in healthcare. EMS and TENS are prominent in healthcare applications. EMS facilitates muscle rehabilitation and posture correction. TENS is used for sensory feedback restoration in limb amputation, electrotactile feedback, and muscle relaxation benefits. TI and vibrotactile haptic systems are also significant, with applications in medical image visualization, rehabilitation, and footwear technology, aiding navigation, fitness tracking, and improving gait and balance. Kinesthetic haptic systems, as seen in a smart shoe, enhance the virtual terrain experience in VR scenarios for rehabilitation. Integrating vibrotactile and kinesthetic haptics can offer efficient training experiences that are especially crucial during events such as the COVID-19 pandemic.

Acknowledgements This research was funded by the joint UAEU-ZU grant no. R22021.

References

1. Collecchia, G.: The declining power of the human touch in the digital world. Recenti Progr. Med. **115**(4), 175–178 (2024)
2. Derpmanns, A.: Meaningful shrinkage. New Electr. **55**(10), 22–27 (2022)
3. Kelly, T., Mottahed, B., Integlia, R.: Advancement in Orthopedics Through an Accessible Wearable Device. International Conference on Human Factors and Wearable Technologies, Washington DC (2020)
4. Kapoor, S., et al.: Haptics: touchfeedback technology widening the horizon of medicine. J. Clin. Diagn. Res. **8**(3), 294–299 (2014)
5. Shazhaev, I., Mihaylov, D., Shafeeg, A.: A review of haptic technology applications in healthcare. Open J. Appl. Sci. **13**, 163–174 (2023)
6. Bortone, I., et al.: Wearable haptics and immersive virtual reality rehabilitation training in children with neuromotor impairments. IEEE Trans. Neural Syst. Rehabil. Eng. **26**, 1469–1478 (2018)
7. Howell, J., et al.: Training for palpatory diagnosis on the virtual haptic back: performance improvement and user evaluations. J. Am. Osteopath. Assn. **108**(1), 29–36 (2008)

8. Kanakamedala, A.C., et al.: Haptic feedback during virtual reality training significantly improves first-year orthopedic resident performance at tibia drilling: a randomized trial. Curr. Orthopaed. Pract. **34**(5), 251–256 (2023)
9. Vaughan, N., Dubey, V.N., Wee, M.Y., Isaacs, R.: Haptic feedback from human tissues of various stiffness and homogeneity. Adv. Robot. Res. **1**(3), 215–237 (2014)
10. Borresen, A., Wolfe, C., Lin, C.K., Tian, Y., Raghuraman, S., Nahrstedt, K., Prabhakaran, B., Annaswamy, T.: Usability of an immersive augmented reality based telerehabilitation system with haptics (ARTESH) for synchronous remote musculoskeletal examination. Int. J. Telerehabil. **11**(1), 23–32 (2018)
11. Minopoulos, G., et al.: A medical image visualization technique assisted with AI-based haptic feedback for robotic surgery and healthcare. Appl. Sci. **13**(3592), 879 (2023)
12. Shull, P., Damian, D.: Haptic wearables as sensory replacement, sensory augmentation and traine. NeuroEng. Rehabil. **12**(59), 326 (2015)
13. Cyberglove: Cyberglove (2023). http://www.cyberglovesystems.com/. Accessed 6 June 2024
14. Motaharifar, M., et al.: Applications of haptic technology, virtual reality, and artificial intelligence in medical training during the COVID-19 pandemic. Front. Robot. AI **8**, 458–965 (2021)
15. Giri, G., Maddahi, Y., Zareinia, K.: An application-based review of haptics technology. Robotics **10**(1), 29 (2021)
16. See, A., Choco, J., Chandramohan, K.: Touch, texture and haptic feedback: a review on how we feel the world around US. Appl. Sci. **12**(4686), 12–31 (2022)
17. Esteban, G., Fernández, C., Conde, M.Á., García-Peñalvo, F.J.: Playing with SHULE: surgical haptic learning environment. In: Proceedings of the Second International Conference on Technological Ecosystems for Enhancing Multiculturality, Salamanca (2014)
18. Zhang, J., et al.: Maxillofacial surgical simulation system with haptic feedback. J. Ind. Manag. Optim. **17**(6), 3645–3657 (2021)
19. Chen, X., Sase, K., Konno, A., Tsujita, T.: Identification of mechanical properties of brain parenchyma for brain surgery haptic simulation, Bali, Indonesia. IEEE Int. Confer. Robot. Biomimet. (2014)
20. Hsieh, M.S., Tsai, M.D., Yeh, Y.D.: An amputation simulator with bone sawing haptic interaction. Biomed. Eng. Appl. Basis Commun. **18**(5), 229–236 (2006)
21. Nguyen, M., et al.: Low-end haptic devices for knee bone drilling in a serious game. World J. Sci. Technol. Sustain. Develop. **14**(2/3), 241–253 (2017)
22. Han, S.W., Sung, S.K., Shin, B.S.: Virtual reality simulation of high tibial osteotomy for medical training. Mobile Inform. Syst. (2022)
23. Berengueres, J., Fritschi, M., McClanahan, R.: A smart pressure-sensitive insole that reminds you to walk correctly: an orthotic-less treatment for over pronation (2014). https://doi.org/10.1109/EMBC.2014.6944127
24. Niroshan: Niroshan (2014). http://niroshan.com/projects/vibrasole. Accessed 14 Oct 2023
25. Otis, M., et al.: Use of an Enactive Insole for Reducing the Risk of Falling on Different Types of Soil Using Vibrotactile Cueing for the Elderly (2016). https://doi.org/10.1371/journal.pone.0162107
26. Sie, A., Boe, D., Rombokas, E.: Design and Evaluation of a Wearable Haptic Feedback System for Lower Limb Prostheses During Stair Descent, pp. 219–224. IEEE, Enschede (2018)
27. Zanotto, D., Turchet, L., Boggs, E.M., Agrawal, S.K.: SoleSound: Towards a Novel Portable System for Audio-tactile Underfoot Feedback. IEEE, São Paulo (2014)
28. Wang, Y., Minor, M.: Design and evaluation of a soft robotic smart shoe for haptic terrain rendering. IEEE/ASME Trans. Mechatr. **23**(6), 2974–2979 (2018)
29. Cesini, I., et al.: Assessment of intuitiveness and comfort of wearable haptic feedback strategies for assisting level and stair walking. Electronics **9**(1676), 352 (2020)
30. Collu, R., et al.: Wearable high voltage compliant current stimulator for restoring sensory feedback (2023). https://doi.org/10.3390/mi14040782
31. Chan, J., Torah, R.: E-textile haptic feedback gloves for virtual and augmented reality applications (2022). https://doi.org/10.3390/engproc2022015001

32. Fidopiastis, C., Rizzo, A., Rolland, J.: User-centered virtual environment design for virtual rehabilitation. J. Neuroeng. Rehabil. **7**(1), 3542 (2010)
33. Plotas, P., et al.: Effects of Transcutaneous Electrical Nervous Stimulation (TENS) on Dysphonic Patients: A Systematic Review Study (2023). https://doi.org/10.3390/medicina5 9101737
34. Cacho, A., Tordera, C., Colmenero, C.: Use of transcutaneous electrical nerve stimulation (TENS) for the recovery of oral function after orthognathic surgery (2022). https://doi.org/10. 3390/jcm11123268
35. Lechal: Lechal (2023). https://www.lechal.com/#Accurate-Fitness-Metrics. Accessed 14 Oct 2023
36. Caserman, P., Krug, C., Göbel, S.: Recognizing full-body exercise execution errors using the teslasuit. Sensors **21**(24), 8389 (2021)
37. Kattoju, R.K., Taranta, E., Ghamandi, R., Laviola, J.J.: Automatic Improper Loading Posture Detection and Correction Utilizing Electrical Muscle Stimulation, pp. 1–18. Association for Computing Machinery, New York (2023).
38. Ramones, A., del-Rio-Guerra, M.: Recent Developments in Haptic Devices Designed for Hearing-Impaired People: A Literature Review (2023). https://doi.org/10.3390/s23062968
39. Ivanova, E., Lorenz, K., Schrader, M., Minge, M.: Developing Motivational Visual Feedback for a New Telerehabilitation System for Motor Relearning After Stroke. Sunderland (2017)
40. Profita, H.P.: Smart garments: an on-body interface for sensory augmentation and substitution. In: Seattle, UbiComp 2014: Adjunct Proceedings of the 2014 ACM International Joint Conference on Pervasive and Ubiquitous Computing (2014).
41. Mehmood, A., Rowther, A.A., Kobusingye, O., Hyder, A.A.: Assessment of pre-hospital emergency medical services in low-income settings using a health systems approach. Int. J. Emerg. Med. **11**(1), 5425 (2018)
42. Kutuk, M.E., Dulger, L.C., Dag, M.T.: Applications on haptic rehabilitation. In: Antalya, 2016 Medical Technologies National Conference, TIPTEKNO (2016)
43. Ouyang, Q., et al.: Bio-inspired haptic feedback for artificial palpation in robotic surgery. IEEE Trans. Biomed. Eng. **68**(10), 3184–3193 (2021)
44. Padilla, J.F., Pitarch, E.P., Sánchez-Suárez, I., Ticó-Falguera, N.: Hand motion analysis during the execution of the action research arm test using multiple sensors. Sensors **22**(9), 598 (2021)
45. Aijaz, A., et al.: The IEEE P1918.1 reference architecture framework for the tactile internet and a case study. In: GLOBECOM 2020–2020 IEEE Global Communications Conference, pp. 1–6. Taipei (2020)
46. Zanotto, D., Turchet, L., Boggs, E.M., Agrawal, S.: SoleSound: towards a novel portable system for audio-tactile underfoot feedback. 5th IEEE RAS/EMBS International Conference on Biomedical Robotics and Biomechatronics. 2014 Aug

Chapter 3
Exploring Haptic Technology's Role in Gaming and Entertainment

Abstract Haptic technology has become synonymous with gaming. From consoles to gloves, vests, and chairs, haptics provides feedback that elevates immersion and engagement. This chapter explores the world of haptics in gaming and entertainment, from rudimentary rumble features to cutting-edge force feedback systems. It examines various haptic applications, including training and learning tasks, motor rehabilitation, entertainment, and gaming for visually impaired users. Additionally, the chapter reviews the different types of haptic feedback, such as vibration, force, wind, and thermal feedback, and their integration into gaming peripherals and virtual reality (VR) devices. The chapter also examines other aspects, such as control and feedback, the weight simulation of virtual objects, emotional response, accessibility, and cinematic experiences.

Keywords Haptics · Gaming · Entertainment

3.1 Introduction

In 2021, the global gaming industry exceeded $300 billion in revenue, driven by the surge in mobile gaming and electronic sports (esports) [1]. On the other hand, in cinema, the global box office revenue is approximately $21 billion [2]. Both industries utilize haptics to increase their entertainment in different ways and with different adoption rates. In gaming, haptics has been increasingly adopted (see Chap. 5 for trend analysis). The main reason is that it is a cost-effective way to improve user experience, usually via the game controller [3, 4]. Haptics also enhances interactivity in virtual environments [5].

From a technological point of view, haptic technology combines the know-how from three fields: computer science, mechanical engineering, and human–computer interaction [6]. Over the past decade, the technology has advanced due to three drivers: (i) robotic teleoperation, (ii) virtual reality (VR), and (iii) augmented reality (AR) [7]. Despite the significant advancement in the past decade, haptic fidelity is comparatively not at the same level of visual fidelity found in VR headsets, smartphones, or TV displays. In other words, a realistic recreation of haptic sensations when a user manipulates objects is not commercially available. A few of these limitations are how rich textures are perceived, how sharply shapes are perceived, the weight range, emulation of the thermal transfer coefficient of various materials, and other properties such as elasticity and plasticity coefficients. The reasons for the lack of haptic fidelity are unfavorable utility cost trade-offs [8, 9]. However, creating a realistic perception of objects is a precondition to believable immersion in a virtual world [10]. Therefore, further advancements in haptics might be needed to reach the same fidelity currently available in visual displays [11].

On the other hand, judging by the high adoption rate in game controllers, the value of adding even low-fidelity haptics seems favorable relative to their comparative cost. Researchers have noted that integrating haptics into gaming devices has reshaped how gamers interact with virtual environments [3, 4] by complementing the visual and auditory stimuli [12]. Further, [13] argued that virtual environments (VEs) without high-fidelity haptics cannot fully immerse the user.

From a historical point of view, haptics in gaming has been marked by various milestones that each have improved the immersion level. From the early adoption of simple vibrotactile effects in console gaming to sophisticated force feedback and tactile sensations in PC gaming [14].

The first milestone was incorporating basic *"rumble"* features, which have since developed into complex systems capable of simulating various textures and forces [15]. Following this, progress was driven by both player demand and market incentives. This led to the widespread adoption of more sophisticated haptic feedback across various gaming platforms [14]. Finally, the development of haptic rendering techniques, which compute the forces exerted on users as they interact with virtual environments, has become central as more compute power and the resolution of available haptics increases [16].

In what follows, we explore the various applications of haptics in gaming and entertainment, highlighting their impact on user engagement and gameplay (Sect. 3.2). We discuss the different types of haptic feedback, including types such as force feedback and vibration feedback. We also examine how each has been implemented in gaming peripherals, VR, AR devices, and mobile platforms (Sect. 3.3). To conclude, we examine the challenges and opportunities for haptics in gaming, including integrating haptic technologies into existing gaming and entertainment ecosystems (Sect. 3.4).

3.2 Applications of Haptics in Gaming and Entertainment

Table 3.1 shows an overview of the applications of haptics in gaming. Haptic technology has been widely used in serious games (i.e., for training purposes). For example, a serious game for training laparoscopic suturing surgery uses a pair of haptic devices [17] to physically model a virtual environment to assess the level of skills developed by the trainees. Several other studies have used haptic-based serious games for motor rehabilitation purposes [18–22].

Serious games have also been used to support visually impaired users. A study proposed using audio plus haptic data exchange to improve the gaming experience for visually impaired individuals [23]. The study presented the HapTech console, which uses a 7 × 4 vibration motor matrix as a user interface for haptic interaction in gameplay. The console conveys game object movements through directional vibrations, while an accompanying LED grid visually represents the vibration matrix. The system is controlled by an Arduino MEGA microcontroller, facilitating the integration of tactile and visual elements in the gaming experience. The console's evaluation showed that audio and haptic interactions combined to create an immersive and

Table 3.1 How haptic technology is used in gaming

Application	Stimulation type	Haptic by user action	Device and reference
Serious games (training)	Force	Graspable	SensAble phantom omni or Novint Falcon [17]
Serious games (inclusivity for visually impaired users)	Vibration	Touchable	HapTech console [23]
	Vibration	Graspable	Audio-haptic game with NOVINT Falcon console [25]
	Vibration	Graspable	Memory game with logitech WingMan Rumblepad tactile controller [24]
Serious games (rehabilitation)	Force	Graspable	Whack-a-mole game with NOVINT Falcon console [26]
	Vibration	Wearable	Haptic TactSuit X40 Vest [27]
Enhanced gameplay mechanics and immersion	Force and thermal	Graspable	SoEs attachable module for hand controller [28]
	Vibration	Graspable/wearable	Po2 system in tablet sleeves or gloves [29]
	Thermal and wind	Graspable	BoEs attachable module for hand controller [3, 4]
	Vibration	Wearable	Skinetic vest [30], bHaptics vest, gloves, and face cover [31]
	TENS and EMS	Wearable	TeslaSuit [32]
Environmental immersion	Force	Touchable	Motion 1 chair [33]

enjoyable gaming experience, fostering enthusiastic engagement and collaborative learning. Another notable example of a serious game for visually impaired users is explained in the works of [24]. The authors developed a game that used a Logitech WingMan Rumblepad as the controller. The game required players to remember and match different vibrations produced by the gamepad's tactile effects. Another study focused on helping visually impaired individuals improve their navigation skills [25]. The researchers used a Falcon haptic device to provide force feedback that enabled users to feel the volume and force of virtual objects. The study demonstrated that this type of haptic interface is just as effective as an audio interface for orientation and mobility purposes.

Serious games have been used in rehabilitation. Tokuyama et al. [26] designed a Whack-a-mole game with the NOVINT Falcon haptic interface device for real-time force simulation in rehabilitation. This simulation promotes brain activation and upper limb exercises. The researchers employed both collision handling and haptic rendering to create a training device with high immersion and a maximum reaction force of 900 g. This approach proved cost-effective, portable, and customizable for various rehabilitation settings.

Haptics in gaming has been shown to enhance gameplay mechanics and immersion. For example, [28] introduced Sword of Elements (SoE), an attachable augmented haptic device to improve player engagement. The device uses force and thermal feedback, including an Arduino Nano breadboard, multiple tactile modules, Bluetooth, and a 12-V battery. Using Unity 5 as the game engine, the device enhances an immersive VR game called "The Ancient Maker." Players experience multisensory haptic feedback during activities such as arrowhead-making (by feeling heat and reaction forces) and shooting arrows. Another example of haptic-based enhanced gameplay mechanics is the application highlighted in [29]. The authors introduced the power of 2 (Po2), a novel haptic technology designed to augment illusive vibrotactile sensations in gesture-based gameplay. Po2 utilizes two vibrating actuators on the hands to create the illusion of tactile motion, allowing for dynamic and animated gaming experiences. The technology uses lightweight and inexpensive actuators embedded in devices such as gloves. Israr et al. [29] presented two configurations: (1) holding a device with two hands and (2) wearing gloves to enable unique animated haptic game experiences. These experiences enhance user engagement through multisensory experiences in virtual and augmented reality environments.

Han et al. [3, 4] created Bits of Elements (BoEs), an attachable VIVE controller and tracker case. BoEs provide an immersive haptic experience, including wind, wetness, heat, and motion feedback. BoEs consist of a module system with five slots for different haptic modules, enabling users to switch between modules and activate multiple bits simultaneously. The authors utilized BoEs for a VR puzzle game, "Island Tales." The game allows players to manipulate natural elements with a wand and experience diverse haptic feedback for each element and game object.

Haptic vests, which use a combination of haptic motors and software to create immersive experiences, have been shown to enhance immersive first-person shooter games by increasing players' in-game awareness and realism [34]. For example, Skinetic Haptic Vest [30] uses 20 voice-coil haptic motors or "HapCoil"—an actuator that can generate subtle vibrations that provide a sensation of the material's texture. This vest spreads over the torso and provides vibrotactile perception, creating various sensations such as rumble, low vibration, and tension. Furthering the technology, the bHaptics Tactsuit vest X-40 [31] uses 40 eccentric rotating mass (ERM) motors. These motors send elaborate haptic vibrations that can be adapted for different VR games. The vest also includes haptic gloves and the Haptics TactVisor, a haptic head-mounted display (HMD). Each glove has 6 motors, one on each finger and one on the wrist. The bHaptics TactVisor has four individually adjustable haptic feedback points on the face using 4 ERM motors. bHaptics Tactsuit vest X-40 has applications in healthcare. For example, a recent study [27] used the haptic vest in the context of serious games for mental illness rehabilitation and therapy for schizophrenia to enhance immersion and perception.

Full-body haptic rendering, which began with military testing in the early 2000s [35], now offers real-time feedback. The Teslasuit [32] is a full-body haptic experience creating sensations from gentle touches to impactful forces using electrotactile sensation. This system uses electromuscle stimulation (EMS) and transcutaneous electrical nerve stimulation (TENS). Equipped with 68 adjustable haptic points and 14 inertial measurement unit sensors, it seamlessly translates real-world movements into the virtual environment. The Teslasuit represents a significant leap in haptic technology for immersive and interactive gaming experiences.

Haptic gaming chairs represent a significant addition to the immersive gaming landscape. Cooler Master's Motion 1 [19] revolutionizes gaming chairs, introducing a D-BOX haptic engine that transforms passive seating into a multisensory experience. It mirrors in-game events with remarkable fidelity, providing sensations such as a tank's rumble or a boat's sway. Its adaptive feedback software dynamically adjusts the intensity and type of haptic sensations in realtime. Beyond individual immersion, Motion 1's versatility extends to enhancing movie experiences and offering accessibility features for visually impaired players.

3.3 Types of Haptics in Gaming and Entertainment

Table 3.2 provides an overview of the types of haptics used in gaming and entertainment. For gamers, a journey into VR extends beyond just visuals and audio. Haptic feedback adds a layer of physical sensations, blurring the lines between the digital world and reality. Several haptic technologies are currently used in commercial gaming and entertainment devices to bring touch to life.

3.3.1 Vibrotactile Stimulation

Vibrotactile stimulation is increasingly integrated into various gaming platforms to enhance user engagement and immersion. For example, Sony's PlayStation 5

Table 3.2 Types of haptics used in gaming

Stimulation type	Device	Actuator type
Vibration	DualShock PS5 controller [36]	Voice-coil actuators
	HapTech [23]	Vibrating motors
	Po2 [29]	Vibrating motors
	Surround Haptic [37]	Vibratory transducers
	AR serious game Jacket [38]	14 brushless vibration actuators
Force	Whack-a-mole game [26]	Three voice-coil actuators. One for each degree of freedom
	Logitech G923 TrueForce racing wheel [39]	Electric brushed motors
	Thrustmaster T-GT II racing wheel [40]	40 W brushless motor
	Haptically augmented foosball [41]	Linear actuator
Vibration and force	HaptX Glove [42]	Microfluidic actuators, pneumatic actuators
Muscle and nerve (EMS and TENS)	Teslasuit [32]	N/A
Thermal	ThermoVR [43]	5 thermal modules
	PneuMod [44]	Thermopneumatic actuators

DualSense controller [36] uses voice-coil motors to deliver vibrations. Like speakers, these motors generate feedback that simulates physical impacts and explosions, thus enriching the player's sense of presence in the virtual environment.

Beyond traditional gaming controllers, innovative devices like the HapTech mobile gaming console, designed by [23], leverage a vibration matrix to facilitate haptic interaction. This interaction is useful for visually impaired users as it provides an alternative sensory input during gameplay. Similarly, Po2 technology utilizes gesture-based illusive tactile sensations in gaming platforms [29]. It consists of two vibrating actuators and provides tactile motion. The device can sense movements and vibrations between hands.

Advancements in haptic feedback are also extending into AR gaming, as demonstrated by [38]. The authors designed an AR serious game prototype with a head-mounted device and a vibrotactile feedback jacket. The game allows players to interact, touch, or fight against characters. Hand-gesture recognition is also used to control various functions within the game. The vibrotactile feedback jacket possesses 14 vibration actuators to provide varied tactile sensations corresponding to in-game interactions with the game characters. The integration of hand-gesture recognition allows for a more intuitive and engaging interaction within the AR environment.

Another innovative application, Surround Haptics, introduced by [37], utilizes a grid of vibratory actuators to deliver continuous tactile sensations across the player's body. This technology can be incorporated into gaming chairs or vests, enhancing the sense of immersion by providing tactile feedback that complements the visual and auditory stimuli of the game.

3.3.2 Mechanical Stimulation

Mechanical stimulation uses motors to provide physical sensations that simulate real-world physical interactions [45]. This type of force feedback offers an immersive and realistic experience by providing a deep level of engagement and a tangible sense of presence in various applications.

Various studies have discussed the use of mechanical stimulation in gaming. For example, [26] developed a virtual whack-a-mole game that uses the Falcon haptic device by Novint Technologies to simulate the feeling of hitting a mole with a hammer. The device can deliver a reaction force of up to 900 g, effectively mimicking the physical impact felt in the real world.

The Logitech G923 TrueForce Racing wheel and the Thrustmaster T-GT II offer advanced force feedback capabilities in car racing simulations [39]. The Logitech G923 operates up to 4000 Hz, allowing for detailed and nuanced force sensations. Similarly, the Thrustmaster T-GT II [40] uses real-time force feedback to eliminate delays, providing instantaneous responses with a powerful 40-W brushless motor for a highly immersive racing experience.

Moreover, [41] demonstrated how force feedback can enhance traditional games like foosball. Their setup involves linear actuators connected to sensor plates under the foosball table. When a player manipulates the rods and hits the ball, the sensors trigger the actuators to tighten the movement of the rods, simulating the resistance and physical interaction typically felt in a non-digital game. This integration of haptic feedback elevates the traditional gameplay experience by introducing realistic physical sensations.

3.3.3 Combination of Mechanical with Vibrotactile Stimulation

The HaptX Glove G1 [42] goes beyond basic vibrations by offering detailed touch feedback, strong force effects, and precise movement tracking. It can mimic textures, shapes, and pressure, making VR gaming feel real. The glove has over 130 feedback points on each hand, where small actuators push the skin up to 2 mm to simulate physical pressure, like touching actual objects. The glove's exotendons, powered by air-driven actuators, can exert up to eight pounds of force on each finger, adding up to 40 lbs. per hand.

3.3.4 Muscle and Nerve Stimulation

The Teslasuit [32] is a full-body outfit that delivers haptic feedback, tracks motion, and monitors biometrics. The suit utilizes EMS and TENS. EMS sends electrical pulses to muscle groups, causing them to contract and relax. These pulses can simulate physical actions like walking, jumping [46], or even the sensation of being hit in a virtual environment [47]. Meanwhile, TENS uses low-voltage currents to stimulate nerves, creating tingling or buzzing sensations that enhance your sense of being in the virtual world. This technology provides nuanced feedback that blurs the real and virtual world lines [48].

3.3.5 Thermal Feedback

Thermal feedback is not only about emulating how users sense the temperature of a material in contact with the skin but also such materials' thermal transfer coefficient. For example, glass and metals transfer heat well; therefore, they feel cold at the beginning of the contact. The effect is the opposite in low heat transfer coefficient materials like wood or plastic). This adds an additional layer of realism to VR experiences. Peiris et al. [43] introduced the ThermoVR, a haptic device that uses heating and cooling elements together with an HMD to elicit thermal sensation in VR applications. ThermoVR features five thermal modules that deliver temperature changes directly to the user's face. These modules can warm (by $+3\ ^{\circ}C$) or cool (by $-3\ ^{\circ}C$) within one second, enhancing the user's perception of temperature in any virtual environment. Note that humans can feel the temperature from contact and the radiation of a surface.

Following similar principles, [44] developed PneuMod, a wearable haptic device that can output pressure, heat, and cold to various body parts without extra coding. This device combines pneumatically actuated silicone bubbles with integrated Peltier devices (a thermoelectric device) to integrate thermal and pneumatic feedback. PneuMod can be configured into various wearable forms, such as sleeves, headbands, and leg wraps.

3.4 Context: Where is It Used?

So far, we have analyzed haptics by application (why) (3.2) and by the principle of actuation (how) (3.3). In this section, we discuss the context (where) where haptics is used in gaming. We focus on use cases where the use of haptics impacts user engagement, emotional impact, or overall satisfaction. Table 3.3 is an overview of by context, stimulation type, and device.

3.4.1 Controller Feedback

Controllers like the Sony DualShock and Xbox One [36] use vibrations to mimic textures, terrain, and game actions. Some, like the PlayStation DualSense controller, feature adaptive triggers that can mimic the resistance of objects in the real world, like the kickback from firing a gun, making the gaming experience more immersive. These triggers work alongside dual actuators, providing more refined feedback than traditional rumble motors.

Table 3.3 An overview of the context of the use of haptics in gaming and entertainment

Context of use	Stimulation type	Device/references
Controller feedback	Vibration	Sony DualSense controller [36]
Virtual object weight simulation	Vibration and force	HaptX Glove [42]
Emotional and physical sensation	TENS and EMS	Teslasuit [32]
	Vibration	bHaptics TactSuit [48]
Accessibility for special-need people (visual and hearing impairment)	Vibration	HapTech console [23]
	Force	Audio-Haptic Game with NOVINT Falcon console [25]
	Vibration	Haptic chair [49]
Virtual environment immersion	Force	Wolverine glove [50]
	Thermal (thermoplastic PE-RT tubes)	Therminator [51]
	Hybrid-haptic feedback system: thermal, wind, and vibrotactile	Sense [52], Haptic Around [53]
	Mechanical and wind	Virtual super-leaping system [54]
Cinematography	Vibration	D-box [33], 4DX [55], Woojer Edge vest [56], and SUBPAC M2 [57]

3.4.2 Virtual Object Weight Simulation

HaptX Gloves [42] are exoskeletons that enhance physical movements, allowing users to experience the weight of virtual objects and physical exertion. HaptX's Airpack generates air quietly and efficiently. It is lightweight enough to wear as a backpack for room-scale use or to be placed on a table without any tethers holding you back. It runs on a 3-h battery for on-the-go movement.

3.4.3 Emotional and Physical Sensation

In 1992, the sense of touch was described as one of the five love languages by G. Chapman. While the experimental data did not corroborate the theory [58], the role of touch in human wellbeing is undisputed. Haptic technology can also convey emotion to amplify narrative impact in gaming and entertainment. For example, haptic suits, such as the Teslasuit [32] and bHaptics TactSuit [48], use vibrations and pressure changes to evoke emotional responses from users. The neuromorphic algorithm in bHaptics gloves enhances the virtual experience by adding sensory elements to every interaction, from pressing buttons, lifting dumbbells, petting cats, and shaking hands to hugging virtual avatars.

3.4.4 Accessibility for Special-Need People

Haptics is instrumental in making gaming and entertainment more accessible to diverse audiences. Haptic feedback devices, such as the HapTech console [23], exchange audio and haptic data between the user and the system for a better gaming experience. The gaming console is designed to be light, portable, easy to use, and reprogrammable to provide the visually impaired with a new source of entertainment. Similarly, [25] developed a video game with audio and haptic interfaces that use virtual environments to stimulate orientation and mobility skills for visually impaired individuals.

Nanayakkara et al. [49] aimed to enrich the music experience for people with hearing impairment by enhancing the sensory input of information via channels other than in-air audio reception by the ear. Instead, the researchers sought to use vibration. They designed a haptic chair to amplify vibrations produced by musical sounds with the help of contact speakers (SolidDrive™ SD1 and Nimzy™ Vibro Max). These contact speakers can attach to most surfaces to vibrate and produce sound.

3.4.5 Virtual Environment Immersion

Haptic devices like the Ultraleap Gemini [59], HaptX gloves [42], and SenseGlove Nova gloves [60] support mm resolution pads that attach to the fingertips. HaptX, for instance, uses a deformable pin matrix driven by air or hydraulic channels etched on silicon. They integrate with VR Unity or Unreal-made games or applications to create more vivid experiences. However, this requires a compressor.

Choi et al. [50] introduced the *Wolverine*, a low-cost, lightweight system for directional braking in haptic applications. This device enables the precise simulation of objects held between the thumb and fingers. It uses brake-based locking sliders that can withstand significant force, consuming minimal energy per interaction. Further enhancing VR immersion, [51] developed the *Therminator*. This device provides thermal feedback by circulating warm or cold liquids, enabling temperature perception. When this feedback is synced with visual stimuli, VR becomes more immersive.

Chou et al. [52] presented *sense,* a 4D audiovisual entertainment system combining scene recognition with haptic feedback. This makes it easy to retrofit haptics to existing content. The system allows users to feel temperature and vibrations corresponding to on-screen events while watching movies at home that were made before haptics was considered, conceivably heightening any movie experience.

Han et al. [53] introduced Haptic Around, a hybrid system that recreates multiple tactile sensations in VR, such as heat, air, and mist. This system supports immersive interactions with elements symbolic of the sun, air, and water, allowing users to explore virtual spaces and experience tactile sensations without direct contact.

Moreover, the concept of virtual Super-Leaping [54] simulates extreme activities like skyjumping by offering synchronized visual, kinesthetic, and airflow feedback through a head-mounted display and a haptic device capable of generating significant force, thus deepening the sense of immersion in virtual environments.

3.4.6 Cinematography

Haptic technology enhances cinematic experiences by synchronizing vibrations and movements with on-screen action. Haptic seats, such as those from D-BOX [33] and 4DX [55], create a more visceral experience for cinemagoers. Haptic vests, like the Woojer Edge vest [56] and SubPac M2 [57], provide full-body immersion with vibrations and air jets, simulating environmental effects.

3.5 Conclusion

Haptics has made gaming experiences more immersive by adding a dimension of sensory modality. This chapter explored the diverse applications of haptics, ranging from basic vibratory feedback in gaming consoles to sophisticated exoskeletons, vests, and suits that further blur the lines between the real and virtual worlds.

The combination of enhanced control and controller feedback provides users with additional information about virtual environments, virtual textures, and in-game actions, enriching gameplay. Haptic gloves enable users to perceive the weight of virtual objects and physical resistance, adding a layer of realism to interactions. Haptic suits leverage vibration and pressure changes to evoke emotional responses, amplifying the narrative impact in games and VR.

For improved accessibility, haptic devices allow visually impaired individuals to engage in gaming through touch-based interfaces. Beyond gaming, haptic technology facilitates realistic manipulation of virtual objects in the entertainment industry, with wristbands combining haptic feedback and visual displays for interactive experiences. In cinematography, haptic seats and vests synchronize vibrations and movements with on-screen action, creating a more visceral and immersive cinematic experience.

Acknowledgements This research was funded by the joint UAEU-ZU grant no. R22021.

References

1. Accenture: Global Gaming Industry Value Now Exceeds $300 Billion, New Accenture Report Finds (2021). https://newsroom.accenture.com/news/2021/global-gaming-industry-value-now-exceeds-300-billion-new-accenture-report-finds. Accessed 31 May 2024
2. Hancock, D., Slee, J., Wunsch-Vincent, S.: Resurgence of Global Cinema: 2022 and 2023 Witness Forceful Comeback But Still Shy of Pre-pandemic Norms (2024). https://www.wipo.int/global_innovation_index/en/gii-insights-blog/2024/global-cinema.html. Accessed 31 May 2024
3. Han, P.-H., et al.: BoEs: Attachable Haptics Bits on Gaming Controller for Designing Interactive Gameplay, pp. 1–2 (2017)
4. Han, P.-H., et al.: BoEs: Attachable Haptics Bits on Gaming Controller for Designing Interactive Gameplay. Bangkok, SIGGRAPH Asia 2017 VR Showcase (2017)
5. Moon, H.S., Orr, G., Jeon, M.: Hand tracking with vibrotactile feedback enhanced presence, engagement, usability, and performance in a virtual reality rhythm game. Int. J. Hum. Comput. Interact. **14**(2840–2851), 39 (2023)
6. Orozco, E.I.M., Luciano, C.J.: Introduction to haptics. In: Comprehensive Healthcare Simulation: Neurosurgery. Comprehensive Healthcare Simulation, pp. 141–151. Springer, Cham (2018)
7. Adilkhanov, A., Rubagotti, M., Kappassov, Z.: Haptic devices: wearability-based taxonomy and literature review. IEEE Access **10**, 91923–91947 (2022)
8. Ding, H., Hino, A., Mitake, H., Hasegawa, S.: Soft! Squishy! Touch with More Soft-bunnies!. Kobe, SIGGRAPH Asia 2015 Haptic Media and Contents Design (2015)

9. Schorr, S.B., Okamura, A.M.: Fingertip tactile devices for virtual object manipulation and exploration. In: ACM SIGCHI Conference on Human Factors in Computing Systems (2017)
10. Cabaret, P.-A., et al.: Does multi-actuator vibrotactile feedback within tangible objects enrich VR manipulation? IEEE Trans. Visual. Comput. Graph. **32**, 1–13 (2023)
11. Sigrist, R., Rauter, G., Riener, R., Wolf, P.: Augmented visual, auditory, haptic, and multimodal feedback in motor learning: a review. Psych. Bull. Rev. **20**, 21–53 (2013)
12. Jeong, S., Yun, H.H., Lee, Y., Han, Y.: Glow the Buzz: a VR Puzzle Adventure Game Mainly Played Through Haptic Feedback. In: Extended Abstracts of the 2023 CHI Conference on Human Factors in Computing Systems (CHI EA '23). Hamburg (2013)
13. Kim, M., Jeon, C., Kim, J.: A study on immersion and presence of a portable hand haptic system for immersive virtual reality. Sensors **17**(5), 1141 (2017)
14. Giri, G., Maddahi, Y., Zareinia, K.: An application-based review of haptics technology. Robotics **10**(1), 29 (2021)
15. Peruvemba, S.: Please, touch the display. Solid State Technol. **60**(2), 10–11 (2017)
16. Laycock, S.D., Day, A.: A Survey of Haptic Rendering Techniques, pp. 50–65. Wiley Online Library (2007)
17. De Paolis, L.T., Ricciardi, F., Giuliani, F.: Development of a Serious Game for Laparoscopic Suture Training, pp. 90–102. Springer (2014)
18. Bortone, I., et al.: Integration of Serious Games and Wearable Haptic Interfaces for Neuro Rehabilitation of Children with Movement Disorders: A Feasibility Study, pp. 1094–1099 (2017)
19. Broeren, J., Sunnerhagen, K.S., Rydmark, M.: Haptic virtual rehabilitation in stroke: transferring research into clinical practice. Phys. Therapy Rev. **14**(5), 322–335 (2009)
20. Gobron, S.C., et al.: Serious Games for Rehabilitation Using Head-Mounted Display and Haptic Devices, pp. 199–219. Springer International Publishing, Lecce (2015)
21. Gutierrez, A., Sepulveda-Munoz, D., Gil-Agudo, A., Guzman, A.R.: Serious game platform with haptic feedback and EMG monitoring for upper limb rehabilitation and smoothness quantification on spinal cord injury patients. Appl. Sci. **10**(3), 963 (2020)
22. Hou, X., Sourina, O.: Emotion-Enabled Haptic-Based Serious Game for Post Stroke Rehabilitation, pp. 31–34 (2013)
23. Walia, A., Goel, P., Kairon, V., Jain, M.: HapTech: Exploring Haptics in Gaming for the Visually Impaired, pp. 1–6 (2020)
24. Raisamo, R., Patomäki, S., Hasu, M., Pasto, V.: Design and evaluation of a tactile memory game for visually impaired children. Interact. Comput. **19**(2), 196–205 (2007)
25. Sánchez, J.: Development of navigation skills through audio haptic videogaming in learners who are blind. Proced. Comput. Sci. **14**, 102–110 (2012)
26. Tokuyama, Y., Rajapakse, R.J., Miya, S., Konno, K.: Development of a Whack-a-Mole Game with Haptic Feedback for Rehabilitation, pp. 29–35. IEEE (2016)
27. Deusdado, L.D., Antunes, A.F.: Virtual reality haptic device for mental illness treatment. Proced. Comput. Sci. **219**, 1112–1119 (2023)
28. Chen, Y.-S., et al.: Soes: Attachable Augmented Haptic on Gaming Controller for Immersive Interaction, pp. 71–72 (2016)
29. Israr, A., et al.: Po2: Augmented Haptics for Interactive Gameplay, pp. 1–1 (2015)
30. Skinetic: Skinetic: Creators Edition (2023). https://www.skinetic.actronika.com/product/ski netic-creators-edition. Accessed 10 June 2024
31. bHaptics: Tactsuit x40 (2024). https://www.bhaptics.com/tactsuit/tactsuit-x40. Accessed 10 June 2024
32. Teslasuit: Teslasuit Dev Kit (2023). https://teslasuit.io/products/teslasuit-4/
33. CoolerMaster: Motion 1 Haptic Gaming Chair (2023). https://www.coolermaster.com/catalog/ setup/chairs/motion-1/
34. SöDerströ, M.U., et al.: Haptic Feedback in First Person Shooter Video Games, pp. 1–6 (2022)
35. Lindeman, R.W., Page, R., Yanagida, Y., Sibert, J.L.: Towards full-body haptic feedback: the design and deployment of a spatialized vibrotactile feedback system. In: VRST '04: Proceedings of the ACM Symposium on Virtual Reality Software and Technology (2004)

36. PlayStation: PlayStation 5 Accessories DualSense Wireless Controller (2024). https://www.playstation.com/en-ae/accessories/dualsense-wireless-controller/
37. Israr, A., Kim, S.-C., Stec, J., Poupyrev, I.: Surround Haptics: Tactile Feedback for Immersive Gaming Experiences. Association for Computing Machinery (2012)
38. Zhu, L., Cao, Q., Cai, Y.: Development of augmented reality serious games with a vibrotactile feedback jacket. Virtual Real. Intell. Hardw. 2(5), 454–470 (2020)
39. Logitech, G.: Logitech G923 TrueForce Racing Wheel (2024). https://www.logitechg.com/en-us/products/driving/g923-trueforce-sim-racing-wheel.html
40. Thrustmaster: T-GT II (2024). https://www.thrustmaster.com/en-us/products/t-gt-ii/
41. Gatti, E., Pittera, D., Moya, J.B., Obrist, M.: Haptic Rules! Augmenting the Gaming Experience in Traditional Games: The Case Of Foosball, pp. 430–435. Munich (2017)
42. Hapt, X.: HaptX Gloves G1 (2024). https://haptx.com/
43. Peiris, R.L., et al.: Thermovr: Exploring Integrated Thermal Haptic Feedback with Head Mounted Displays, pp. 5452–5456 (2017)
44. Zhang, B., Sra, M.: Pneumod: A Modular Haptic Device with Localized Pressure and Thermal Feedback, pp. 1–7 (2021)
45. Rekimoto, J.: Traxion: a tactile interaction device with virtual force sensation. In: ACM SIGGRAPH 2014 Emerging Technologies, SIGGRAPH 2014 (2014)
46. Nith, R., et al.: DextrEMS: increasing dexterity in electrical muscle stimulation by combining it with brakes. In: The 34th Annual ACM Symposium on User Interface Software and Technology (UIST '21) (2021)
47. Lopes, P., Ion, A., Baudisch, P.: Impacto: simulating physical impact by combining tactile stimulation with electrical muscle stimulation. In: Proceedings of the 28th Annual ACM Symposium on User Interface Software and Technology (UIST '15) (2015)
48. Teslasuit: Teslasuit-4 (2024). https://teslasuit.io/products/teslasuit-4/. Accessed 31 May 2024
49. Nanayakkara, S., Taylor, E., Wyse, L., Ong, S.H.: An Enhanced Musical Experience for the Deaf: Design and Evaluation of a Music Display and a Haptic Chair, pp. 337–346 (2009)
50. Choi, I., et al.: Wolverine: A Wearable Haptic Interface for Grasping in Virtual Reality. IEEE, pp. 986–993 (2016)
51. Günther, S., et al.: Therminator: Understanding the Interdependency of Visual and On-Body Thermal Feedback in Virtual Reality, pp. 1–14. Association for Computing Machinery, New York (2020)
52. Chou, C.-H., et al.: Design of desktop audiovisual entertainment system with deep learning and haptic sensations. Symmetry 12(10), 1718 (2020)
53. Han, P.-H., et al.: Haptic Around: Multiple Tactile Sensations for Immersive Environment and Interaction in Virtual Reality, pp. 1–10 (2018)
54. Sasaki, T., et al.: Virtual super-leaping: Immersive extreme jumping in VR. In: Proceedings of the 10th Augmented Human International Conference 2019 (AH2019), pp. 1–8 (2019)
55. Sharp, J.: 4DX: Here Come the Feelies (2014). https://www2.bfi.org.uk//news/sightsound/4dx-here-come-the-feelies. Accessed 13 April 2024
56. Woojer: Freakin' Amazing Sensations (2024). https://www.woojer.com. Accessed 13 April 2024
57. SUBPAC: Subpac M2 (2024). https://subpac.com/subpac-m2/. Accessed 13 April 2024
58. Egbert, N.: Speaking the language of relational maintenance: a validity test of Chapman's five love languages. Commun. Res. Rep. 23(1), 19–26 (2006)
59. Ultraleap: Turning Ultrasound into Virtual Touch (2024). https://www.ultraleap.com/haptics/. Accessed 4 May 2024
60. SenseGlove: The New Sense in VR for Enterprise (2024). https://www.senseglove.com/product/nova/. Accessed 4 May 2024

Chapter 4
Challenges of Designing Haptic Experiences

Abstract Haptic technology holds immense promise for enriching user experiences in various fields. However, designing effective haptic solutions is not without challenges. This chapter explores the complexities surrounding haptic technology development, covering both general design challenges and those specific to different applications. Based on our research, it is still very difficult to strike a balance between affordability and accuracy. Making trade-offs between accuracy, size, power consumption, and adaptability is frequently necessary when designing a haptic device. Further complicating the development process is the absence of strong tools and established guidelines for creating haptic experiences. Across various applications, challenges include ensuring precise feedback, user comfort, and standardized interfaces. In healthcare, for example, replicating touch for conditions like overpronation necessitates real-time detection of subtle movements and personalized feedback. Robotics requires realistic, low-latency feedback for natural human–robot interaction, while industrial applications prioritize design complexity, feedback quality, cost-effectiveness, and operational safety.

Keywords Haptics · Design · Challenges

4.1 Introduction

Haptic technology is used in many industries to improve the user experience (UX) in industries like healthcare [1], gaming [2], and automobiles [3]. No matter the industry, simulating the sense of touch with high fidelity remains an engineering challenge. This challenge stems from our skin's intricate network of receptors that respond not only to pressure but also to texture (through vibration sensing) and temperature [4]. Additionally, human perception quirks, capability, sensibility, and preferences about the sense of touch show as much variation as the sense of sight, hearing, and smell [5]. In particular, perception and interpretation at the cognitive level are specifically affected in the case of touch by (1) the variation in the shape of human fingertips [6],

© The Author(s), under exclusive license to Springer Nature Switzerland AG 2024
M. A. Kuhail et al., *Advances, Applications and the Future of Haptic Technology*,
SpringerBriefs in Computer Science, https://doi.org/10.1007/978-3-031-70588-5_4

(2) individual interpretations and appreciations of haptic effects [7], and (3) aging [8].

Achieving accurate representations of real-world touch without sacrificing computational efficiency or affordability is the most significant barrier to adopting haptics [9]. On a system thinking level, adoption is also hindered by operational factors such as inconsistencies across hardware platforms and slow responsiveness [10], which can result in a poor haptic experience.

Another common challenge is a lack of adequate tools and established practices for designing multisensory experiences with haptics. Designers suffer from a lack of established practices for designing, let alone evaluating the performance of a haptic device [11]. A recent study found that haptic designers face a multitude of challenges [12], including the cost associated with demos, the difficulty in creating design iterations, and the constraints associated with evaluation methods.

Although haptic technology has potential in healthcare, robotics, and industrial applications, several challenges remain. In health wearables, for instance, accurately detecting the overpronation of the foot from pressure sensors requires precise real-time and customization of algorithms [13]. Similarly, user-facing robotic applications require low latency and effective feedback if such feedback is to be perceived as natural [14]. In the same vein, industrial robotic applications also face the same challenges as consumer-facing applications of balancing design complexity, feedback quality, cost-effectiveness, and operational safety [15].

This chapter covers various challenges in applying haptics. We first cover engineering design aspects (Sect. 4.2), including how to achieve high-fidelity haptics. Thereafter, we cover application-based aspects (Sect. 4.3), including healthcare, robotics, and gaming. Finally, we provide a conclusion (Sect. 4.4).

4.2 Design Aspects of Haptic Interfaces

4.2.1 How to Achieve High Fidelity Haptics

Perhaps the biggest challenge for haptic devices stems from having to replicate a realistic sense of touch due to the complexity and sensitivity of human skin [16]. While developers strive to create haptic systems that accurately represent real-world tactile sensations, the computational power and hardware complexity required to achieve this level of fidelity often translate into high costs. According to [9], one of the most significant challenges facing the widespread adoption of haptic technology lies in striking a balance between accuracy and affordability. Similarly, [17] highlight that designing haptic feedback systems for touchscreens presents the challenge of balancing simplicity and accuracy. Like the widespread adoption of basic vibrators in devices like phones and game controllers, cost-effectiveness and user-friendliness are crucial for widespread adoption. However, unlike these simple systems, haptic devices seek to evoke a wide range of tactile sensations, replicating the richness of human touch perception. As such, combining multiple actuators to generate diverse stimuli like forces, vibrations, shapes, and temperatures might seem like the obvious solution, but it can lead to significant technical complexity [18]. In education, building haptic devices requires the challenging task of balancing affordability, student-proof durability, and the ability to create realistic virtual environments [19].

Researchers and designers are addressing the need to improve the accuracy of haptic technology. For example, they have developed flexible, soft-wearable devices that conform to the user's body, minimizing discrepancies caused by shape mismatch [16]. Additionally, researchers are refining device performance through calibration procedures and novel evaluation techniques, aiming to bridge the gap between measured values and the actual physical sensations experienced by users [20].

Designing effective haptic devices often involves navigating a complex web of trade-offs. Striking a balance between seemingly contradictory requirements is crucial: a device needs to be stiff enough to provide realistic force feedback yet lightweight enough for smooth movement [21]. A large workspace allows for a wider range of motion, but a smaller size is more practical. Additionally, powerful actuators capable of delivering strong and accurate sensations often come at a higher cost. Beyond these trade-offs, design processes entail carefully selecting the actuator type, driving mechanism, and the ability to deliver forces in multiple directions (degrees of freedom) [22]. Addressing these challenges effectively requires meticulous engineering and optimization to balance the final haptic device's performance, affordability, and user experience.

4.2.2 Adaptability

Haptics wearables have been developed to be adaptable above all things. To deliver sensation effectively, actuators in wearable haptics must closely conform to the user's body, making size adaptability crucial [4]. This means designing systems that account for skin stretch and deformations during use. Another significant challenge is the need for haptics, particularly those embedded in hand-held devices, to be compact [23]. As such, the haptic device needs to be capable of rendering diverse feedback modalities like thermal sensations, pressure, vibration, texture, and even skin stretch. Furthermore, the rendered sensations must be easily distinguishable and intuitive for users, minimizing the users' need for extensive training.

4.2.3 Tools and Guidelines for Designing Haptic Experiences

Engineers and interaction designers often face a significant hurdle: the lack of robust tools and established guidelines for effectively designing these experiences [11]. Although some general guidance can apply to tactile and haptic interactions, no existing resources provide detailed guidance relating to the particulars of tactile and haptic interactions. Current tools often fall short in facilitating collaboration and exploration, hindering communication and knowledge sharing between designers and stakeholders throughout the development process [24]. However, the field is actively addressing these limitations. Research efforts are exploring new design methods and tools specifically tailored for crafting haptic user interfaces. Studies have evaluated existing approaches and led to the creation of tools like Feelix, a dedicated platform for authoring haptic experiences [25]. Furthermore, workshops and collaborative efforts are crucial in establishing haptics as a unified design discipline [26]. These platforms provide a common ground for designers to share insights, discuss challenges, and propose an agenda for advancing the field.

4.3 Application-Based Challenges of Haptic Technology

Table 4.1 provides an overview of the challenges of developing haptic technology in various fields. The following subsections explore these challenges' specific details and intricacies within each application area.

4.3.1 Healthcare

Although a large literature base addresses the promises of haptics, this is largely limited to applications other than healthcare or specific healthcare applications such as teleoperation. Some researchers remain skeptical due to concerns about patient safety, the ability to replicate realistic haptic feedback during procedures accurately, and the affordability of such devices [28]. Additionally, precise control over haptic devices as well as ensuring proper training for medical professionals, are crucial aspects that need further investigation.

Let's take overpronation as an example of these concerns. Implementing tactile feedback solutions for overpronation, the excessive inward rolling of the foot during movement [13], presents several challenges. Firstly, accurately detecting overpronation in real time requires reliable sensors that capture foot motion and orientation with high precision and accuracy. Detecting subtle changes in foot position and movement associated with overpronation is crucial for providing effective tactile feedback. Additionally, overpronation varies among individuals in severity, gait pattern, and biomechanics, making detecting these variances crucial.

Integrating haptics into medical training simulators presents a delicate balancing act [27]. Any training of complex surgeries on soft tissue needs to have high dexterity, compactness, and responsiveness [41]. While the cost of general-purpose force feedback devices has decreased, custom solutions needed for specific procedures remain expensive. Additionally, the development of realistic tactile interfaces is still in its early stages. Balancing fidelity with affordability is crucial, as multipurpose devices

Table 4.1 An overview of application-based challenges of applying haptics

Application	Challenges
Healthcare [27–30]	• Cost and accessibility • Surgical ergonomics • Integration with medical devices • Clinical validation • Motor learning and skill acquisition • User interface design • Adaptability to patient progress
Navigation and fitness tracking [31, 32]	• Accuracy and precision • Power consumption • Safety and reliability • Environmental factors • Wearability
Robotics [28, 33, 34]	• Sensing and perception • Manipulation and grasping • Energy efficiency • Fault tolerance and robustness • Teleoperation and remote control • Human–robot interaction
Space [35, 36]	• Microgravity • Limited space and weight constraints • Power consumption • Real-time communication
Gaming and virtual reality [4, 37]	• Realism and immersion • Compatibility and integration • Cost and accessibility • User experience design
Consumer electronics [38, 39]	• Miniaturization • Power efficiency • Cost-effectiveness • Durability and reliability • Compatibility and integration
Industrial [15, 40]	• Reliability and durability • Safety compliance • Scalability and cost-effectiveness

offer better software support but might compromise realism compared to custom-built ones. However, ongoing algorithms and software optimization research aims to improve performance and fidelity, even with more affordable haptic solutions.

Haptic technology holds promise for aiding lower-limb amputees with walking, but it still struggles to meet their unique needs. Some key challenges include the time and training required for amputees to adapt to haptic feedback systems, especially if they have not used assistive technologies before [29]. Moreover, making the feedback convenient, easy to understand, and user-friendly are important factors affecting the adoption rate and long-term use.

Integrating haptics into voice therapy for individuals with voice disorders or difficulties related to pitch, volume, and resonance presents distinct challenges [30]. Voice therapy traditionally relies heavily on auditory and visual feedback. Introducing haptic feedback as an additional sensory modality may pose challenges in how users effectively interpret and integrate this new information form into their vocal training. Furthermore, in voice therapy, designing haptic feedback systems that can be personalized and adapted to the specific needs of each patient is crucial to optimize the effectiveness of this intervention [42].

4.3.2 Navigation and Fitness Tracking Applications

Haptic technology offers promising opportunities to enhance user experiences while improving both safety and effectiveness in navigation and fitness-tracking applications, as discussed in [31]. However, a crucial aspect is the accuracy and precision of haptic feedback. Users rely on this feedback for reliable guidance in navigation and fitness tracking. Delivering timely and accurate haptic cues, especially in dynamic environments, can be challenging due to the difficulty of tracking user movements. Moreover, the power consumption of actuators can be high, thus reducing the battery life of navigation and fitness-tracking devices [32]. As such, maintaining device use between recharges requires balancing energy efficiency and haptic feedback quality.

4.3.3 Robotics

Haptic technology in robotics offers a more natural, intuitive approach [33]. However, there are still several significant obstacles. Accurately replicating the full range of human touch, especially for delicate tasks, requires precise force feedback and safety mechanisms [28]. Additionally, haptic feedback needs minimal latency for a natural human–robot connection [14].

Technical considerations include meticulous design to ensure the feedback aligns with real-world sensations. Haptic devices can be power-hungry, demanding a balance between rich feedback and energy efficiency [9]. Adapting feedback to diverse environments necessitates advanced algorithms.

Human factors also play a role. Therefore, haptic cues need to be user-centric—as user perception of these cues should guide the design of feedback that appeals to human sense [34]. Haptic devices in robotics need to be durable, and users require training to interpret and respond to feedback effectively.

Finally, the lack of standardized interfaces can lead to interoperability issues [34]. Scaling haptic feedback to larger robots presents challenges, and balancing affordability with performance is crucial.

4.3.4 Space

To date, the integration of haptic devices into space tasks [35] has been impaired by the specific conditions and constraints that are an intrinsic part of space missions. Microgravity conditions profoundly change the perception of forces [43]. In space, we cannot rely on gravitational loading, and the sensation of tactile resistance needs to be recreated with new mechanisms while maintaining realism.

Moreover, space missions often have limitations on mass, power consumption, or available space, [36], as do all missions slated for deep space. The constraining conditions of space—with extreme temperatures, high radiation levels, and vacuum conditions [44]—also means that haptic devices must be uniquely crafted to withstand these conditions and function reliably without degrading. Standard electronics susceptible to space radiation might not be suitable, and alternatives to standard components might need to be specially developed, making them difficult to source later on [45]. Extreme temperature variations can disrupt haptic feedback devices that use hydraulic and pneumatic systems [46].

4.3.5 Gaming and Virtual Reality

The evolution of haptic technology has already changed how people play games and immerse themselves in virtual reality experiences forever [37]. Expensive high-quality haptic devices [4] create accessibility limitations, while the lack of standardization in devices and interfaces leads to compatibility issues across different platforms, making it difficult to use haptic technology seamlessly [47]. Additionally, powerful haptic feedback often requires significant energy consumption, adding another layer of complexity [48].

Designing comfortable and compact haptic devices without hindering gameplay has proved challenging. Bulky or cumbersome devices can negatively impact user enjoyment [49]. Latency must be minimal for a natural feel [50], and developers must carefully integrate haptic cues with visuals and audio. Replicating a complete range of tactile sensations, like textures and temperatures, remains a work in progress [4]. Customization options and high-resolution feedback are crucial for a detailed and engaging experience but can be difficult to achieve. Finally, ensuring user comfort during extended VR sessions with haptic devices requires careful design considerations [4].

4.3.6 Consumer Electronics

Haptic technology is enriching user experiences in consumer electronics [38]. Currently, almost all mobile phones and smartwatches have vibration feedback functions. However, there are challenges in rendering diversified tactile features such as friction and textures accurately [23]. Achieving high-fidelity sensations and ensuring consistent experiences across devices also remains challenging. Further, customization for individual preferences and diverse needs adds further complexity [39]. Long-term user satisfaction relies on durable and reliable haptic mechanisms and the need to tailor feedback to user preferences and cultural sensitivities.

4.3.7 Industrial Applications

Unique challenges are encountered by industrial applications of haptic technology as well [15]. Despite substantial improvements in hardware and software systems in the last 20 years [40], most haptic technology for product design and manufacturing simulation remains in the research prototype stage, limiting its wider industrial application. Key areas for improvement include design complexity, feedback quality, cost-effectiveness, and operational safety [15, 51]. Designing a haptic interface for industrial use is a complicated interdisciplinary mission requiring consideration of numerous functional specifications, which often overlap with each other in terms of performance requirements. Furthermore, developing scalable haptic interfaces, control algorithms, and network architectures that can support multiple users, devices, and applications is essential.

On the hardware side, ideal haptic devices must meet requirements like large workspaces, strong force and torque feedback, and flexibility. Unfortunately, commercially available devices often fall short in these areas, prompting the development of custom solutions like the HapticGear [52], LHIfAM [53], and iFeel6-BH1500 [54].

4.4 Conclusion

Despite advancements, haptic technology faces challenges in replicating the intricate human sense of touch. Balancing accuracy with affordability remains a key challenge. Effective haptic devices often require trade-offs: realism versus cost, size versus power consumption, and specialization versus adaptability to diverse applications. Ensuring accurate feedback, user comfort, and standardized interfaces are challenges that are common to all fields. Medical applications, like overpronation detection, require real-time detection of minute moves. Similar challenges occur in robotics, where it is critical to accurately simulate the full range of human touch with minimal latency. Haptic feedback in robotics also needs to be robust and consider user perception and training. The industry actively looks for answers through developments in software and hardware by emphasizing user experience, affordability, and accuracy.

Overcoming these challenges is essential to unlock haptic technology's full potential across various industries. Haptic technology can be crucial in diverse fields, from medical training to immersive gaming, balancing accuracy, affordability, and user experience. As the field matures, we can expect haptic technology to become more accessible, user-friendly, and capable of delivering a wider range of realistic tactile sensations.

Acknowledgements This research was funded by the joint UAEU-ZU grant no. R22021.

References

1. Escobar-Castillejos, D., et al.: A review of simulators with haptic devices for medical training. J. Med. Syst. **40**(4), 546 (2016)
2. Deng, S., Chang, J., Zhang, J.J.: A survey of haptics in serious gaming. In: Games and Learning Alliance: Second International Conference, GALA 2013 (2013)
3. Gaffary, Y., Lécuyer, A.: The use of haptic and tactile information in the car to improve driving safety: a review of current technologies. Front. ICT **5**, 5486 (2018)
4. Wee, C., Yap, K.M., Lim, W.N.: Haptic interfaces for virtual reality: challenges and research directions. IEEE Access **9**, 112145–112162 (2021)
5. Lofvenberg, J., Johansson, R.: Regional differences and interindividual variability in sensitivity to vibration in the glabrous skin of the human hand. Brain Res. **301**(1), 65–72 (1984)
6. Malvezzi, M., Chinello, F., Prattichizzo, D., Pacchierotti, C.: Design of personalized wearable haptic interfaces to account for fingertip size and shape. IEEE Trans. Hapt. **14**(2), 266–272 (2021)
7. Seifi, H., MacLean, K.E.: A first look at individuals' affective ratings of vibrations. In: Proceedigns of the 2013 World Haptics Conference (WHC) (2013)
8. Stevens, J., Choo, K.: Spatial acuity of the body surface over the life span. Somatosens. Mot. Res.. Mot. Res. **13**(2), 153–166 (1996)
9. Edwards, J.: Touching research: haptics and signal processing. IEEE Sig. Process. Mag. **31**(2), 11–14 (2014)
10. Kaaresoja, T., Brewster, S., Lantz, V.: Towards the temporally perfect virtual button: touch-feedback simultaneity and perceived quality in mobile touchscreen press interactions. ACM Trans. Appl. Percept. **11**(2), 1–25 (2014)
11. Seifi, H., et al.: How do novice hapticians design? A case study in creating haptic learning environments. IEEE Trans. Hapt. **13**(4), 791–805 (2020)
12. Schneider, O., MacLean, K., Swindells, C., Booth, K.: Haptic experience design: What hapticians do and where they need help. Int. J. Hum. Comput. Stud.Comput. Stud. **107**, 5–21 (2017)
13. Berengueres, J., Fritschi, M., McClanahan, R.: A Smart Pressure-Sensitive Insole that Reminds You to Walk Correctly: An Orthotic-Less Treatment for Over Pronation (2014). https://doi.org/10.1109/EMBC.2014.6944127
14. Muradore, R., Fiorini, P.: A review of bilateral teleoperation algorithms riccardo muradore and paolo fiorini. Acta Polytech. Hung. **13**(1), 191–208 (2016)

15. Hannaford, B., Ryu, J.-H.: Time-domain passivity control of haptic interfaces. IEEE Trans. Robot. Autom.Autom. **18**(1), 1–10 (2002)
16. See, A.R., Choco, J.A.G., Chandramohan, K.: Touch, texture and haptic feedback: a review on how we feel the world around US. Appl. Sci. **12**(9), 4686 (2022)
17. Costes, A., et al.: Towards haptic images: a survey on touchscreen-based surface haptics. IEEE Trans. Hapt. **13**(3), 530–541 (2020)
18. Ernst, M., Banks, M.: Humans integrate visual and haptic information in a statistically optimal fashion. Nature **415**(6870), 429–433 (2002)
19. Martinez, M.O., et al.: 3-D printed haptic devices for educational applications. In: Proceedigns of the 2016 IEEE Haptics Symposium (HAPTICS) (2016)
20. Frad, M., Maaref, H., Otmane, S., Mtibaa, A.: A hybrid optical–mechanical calibration procedure for the Scalable-SPIDAR haptic device. Virtual Real. **21**(3), 109–125 (2017)
21. Torabi, A., et al.: Kinematic design of linkage-based haptic interfaces for medical applications: a review. Prog. Biomed. Eng. **3**(2), 32–54 (2021)
22. Lim, B., Kim, K., Oh, S.-R., Hwang, D.: HaptiCube: a compact 5-DoF finger-wearable tactile interface. In: IEEE/RSJ International Conference on Intelligent Robots and Systems (IROS) (2019)
23. Dangxiao, W., et al.: Haptic display for virtual reality: progress and challenges. Virtual Real. Intell. Hardw. **1**(1), 136–162 (2019)
24. Schneider, O., Maclean, K.: Improvising design with a Haptic Instrument. In: IEEE Haptics Symposium, HAPTICS 2014 (2014)
25. van Oosterhout, A., Hoggan, E., Bruns, M.: Adjustable graphical notation and accessible hardware to accommodate the force feedback design process: redesign of feelix based on preliminary evaluations of design tools and methods. In: Proceedings of the 2022 Nordic Human-Computer Interaction Conference (NordiCHI '22) (2022)
26. Schneider, O., et al.: Sustainable haptic design: improving collaboration, sharing, and reuse in haptic design research. In: Virtual, Conference on Human Factors in Computing Systems—Proceedings (2022)
27. Coles, T.R., Meglan, D., John, N.W.: The role of haptics in medical training simulators: a survey of the state of the art. IEEE Trans. Hapt. **4**(1), 51–66 (2011)
28. Enayati, N., De Momi, E., Ferrigno, G.: Haptics in robot-assisted surgery: challenges and benefits. IEEE Rev. Biomed. Eng. **9**, 49–65 (2016)
29. Fan, R.E., et al.: A haptic feedback system for lower-limb prostheses. IEEE Trans. Neural Syst. Rehabil. Eng.Rehabil. Eng. **16**(3), 270–277 (2008)
30. McLaughlin, M., et al.: Integrated Voice and Haptic Support for Tele-rehabilitation, pp. 590–595. IEEE (2006)
31. Adams, R.J., Hannaford, B.: Stable haptic interaction with virtual environments. IEEE Trans. Robot. Autom.Autom. **15**(3), 465–474 (1999)
32. Yin, J., Hinchet, R., Shea, H., Majidi, C.: Wearable soft technologies for haptic sensing and feedback. Adv. Funct. Mater.Funct. Mater. **31**(39), 2007428 (2021)
33. Albani, J.M., Lee, D.I.: Virtual reality-assisted robotic surgery simulation. J. Endourol.Endourol. **21**(3), 285–287 (2007)
34. Sreelakshmi, M., Subash, T.: Haptic technology: a comprehensive review on its applications and future prospects. Mater. Today Proceed. **4**(2), 4182–4187 (2017)
35. Kennedy, J.M., Gabias, P., Heller, M.A.: Space, haptics and the blind. Geoforum **23**(2), 175–189 (1992)
36. Khan, S.U.E., et al.: Space Physiology and Technology: Musculoskeletal Adaptations, Countermeasures, and the Opportunity for Wearable Robotics (2024). arXiv preprint arXiv:2404.03363
37. Kim, M., Jeon, C., Kim, J.: A study on immersion and presence of a portable hand haptic system for immersive virtual reality. Sensors **17**(5), 1–18 (2017)
38. Kuhail, M.A., et al.: Haptic systems: trends and lessons learned for haptics. Electronics **12**, 1–27 (2023)

39. Seim, C., et al.: Towards haptic learning on a smartwatch. In: Proceedings of the 2018 ACM International Symposium on Wearable Computers, pp. 228–229 (2018)

40. Xia, P.: Haptics for product design and manufacturing simulation. IEEE Trans. Hapt. **9**(3), 358–375 (2016)

41. Verma, V., Chowdary, V., Gupta, M.K., Mondal, A.K.: IoT and robotics in healthcare. In: Medical Big Data and Internet of Medical Things, pp. 245–269. CRC Press (2018)

42. Nanayakkara, S., Wyse, L., Taylor, E.A.: The Haptic Chair as a Speech Training Aid for the Deaf, pp. 405–410 (2012)

43. Hariom, S.K., et al.: Animal physiology across the gravity continuum. Acta Astron. **178**, 522–535 (2021)

44. Dilillo, L., Bosser, A., Javanainen, A., Virtanen, A.: Space radiation effects in electronics. In: Rad-Hard Semiconductor Memories, pp. 1–64 (2018)

45. Kuhnhenn, J., Höffgen, S., Metzger, S., Steffens, M.: Future radiation testing: adapt or fail. In: Proceedings of the International Astronautical Congress, IAC (2018)

46. Kumar, L., Krishnadas Nair, C.: Current trends of additive manufacturing in the aerospace industry. In: Wimpenny, D., Pandey, P., Kumar, L. (eds.) Advances in 3D Printing and Additive Manufacturing Technologies, pp. 39–54. Springer, Singapore (2017)

47. Liu, X., Dohler, M., Mahmoodi, T., Liu, H.: Challenges and opportunities for designing tactile codecs from audio codecs. In: Oulu, EuCNC 2017: European Conference on Networks and Communications (2017)

48. Mills, N., Mills, E.: Taming the energy use of gaming computers. Energy Effic. **9**(2), 321–338 (2016)

49. Teng, S.-Y.: Enabling haptic experiences anywhere, anytime. In: Conference on Human Factors in Computing Systems—Proceedings (2023)

50. Pott, P.P.: Haptic interfaces. In: Manfredi, L. (ed.) Endorobotics: Design, R&D and Future Trends, pp. 257–274. Elsevier (2022)

51. Shanmugam, M., et al.: A comprehensive review of haptic gloves: advances, challenges, and future directions. In: Second International Conference on Electronics and Renewable Systems (ICEARS) (2023)

52. Hirose, M., et al.: HapticGEAR: The Development of a Wearable Force Display System for Immersive Projection Displays, pp. 123–129. IEEE (2001)

53. Borro, D.A.S.J., et al.: A large haptic device for aircraft engine maintainability. IEEE Comput. Graph. Appl.Comput. Graph. Appl. **24**(6), 70–74 (2004)

54. Chen, Z., et al.: iFeel6-BH1500: A Large-Scale 6-DOF Haptic Device, pp. 121–125. IEEE (2012)

Chapter 5
Haptic Technology Adoption and Future Trends

Abstract This chapter investigates how haptic technology has evolved over the last six decades to aid planners and forecasters with their technology roadmapping activities. It presents and reviews data from two case studies that are central to haptic development: (i) the adoption of haptics in personal communication devices (pagers, smartphones, and laptops) and (ii) the adoption of haptics in the automobile industry. The findings highlight the varying speeds and factors that influence the diffusion and adoption of haptics across different devices, industries, and use cases. Then, this information is contextualized using several foresight frameworks, such as technology diffusion theory and gap matrix analysis. The gap matrix analysis details the prevalence of haptic technology across diverse application domains and identifies gaps in commercialization. Finally, the chapter analyzes intellectual property trends in the health, gaming, and automotive sectors, providing a chronological account of patent activity data to track the advancement and cross-domain diffusion of haptic innovations.

Keywords Haptics · Adoption · Tends · Electronics · Automobiles

5.1 Introduction

As a business, haptics is predicted to grow above the global average GDP, which stands at 2.7% (Fig. 5.1). In 2022, the global haptic technology market was worth USD 8.78 billion. According to Precedence Research [1], haptic technology is predicted to rerate 25.04 billion by 2032, growing at a compounded annual growth rate (CAGR) rate of 11.05% [1]—a growth rate exceeding the global GDP. This growth can be attributed to smartphones, tablets, and wearables. Additionally, the gaming industry is also a large consumer of haptics.

The decision to include or exclude a haptic feature in a product ultimately boils down to its economic value or utility [2]. We can use the adoption rate, defined as units sold in a year incorporating haptics, to gauge the technology's diffusion. At present, the adoption rate in areas such as medical training systems [3] and robotic surgery

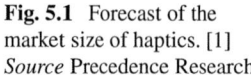

Fig. 5.1 Forecast of the market size of haptics. [1] *Source* Precedence Research

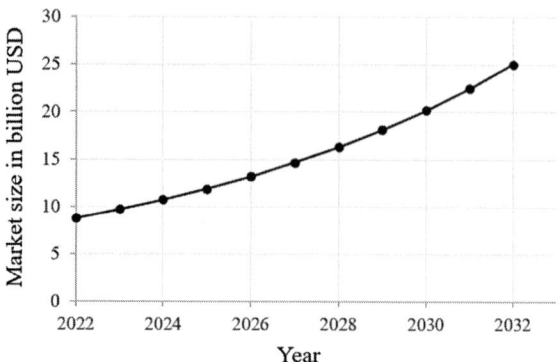

systems [4] remains low due to unfavorable cost–benefit trade-offs [5]. In other areas, such as aerospace, adoption rates also remain limited, but for other reasons: precise and stable spacecraft attitude control necessitates minimizing all vibrations within the craft [6].

This chapter examines the adoption of haptics within two product lines: personal communication devices (pagers, smartphones, laptops) and the automobile. The purpose is to gain insights useful for future planners and technology forecasting. These two product lines have been chosen because of their mass adoption, impact on society, and data availability. This chapter also discusses intellectual property trends in haptic devices in health, gaming, and automobiles. These patents are sorted from oldest to newest to analyze chronologically the advancement of haptics and technology diffusion from one domain to an adjacent domain.

5.2   A Case Study of Haptics Adoption in Personal Communication Devices

In this section, we examine how adoption rates of haptics evolved within the personal communication device industry, taking a case study of Personal Communication Devices (PCD) as a representative. The goal is to extrapolate the adoption patterns and trends to other verticals to help in foresight and technology planning activities. Within PCD, we look at four consecutive product hits: pagers (covering from 1962 to 1995), mobile phones (focusing on years 1997–1999, including smartphones), and laptops (2008–2024). Figure 5.2 shows a summary of the adoption rates of haptics.

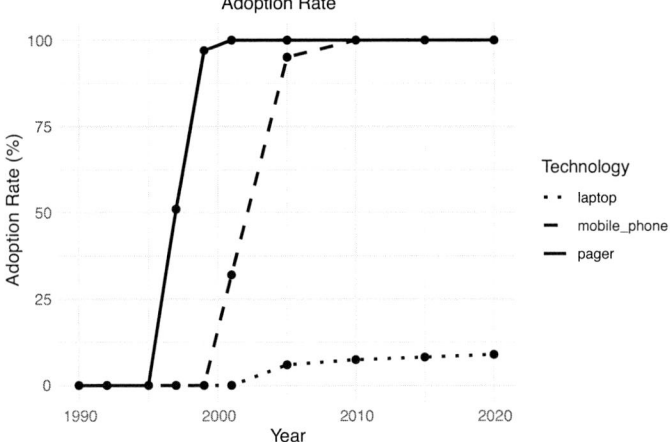

Fig. 5.2   Adoption curve of haptics for smartphones and laptops. [7] *Source* Wikipedia and own estimates from a known market share of several products and brands

5.2.1   The Pager

Early Development and Initial Adoption (1962–1986)

The history of haptic technology in pagers begins with the early models that lacked vibration capabilities. In the United States (US), the first pagers, such as the BellBoy in 1962 and the Motorola Pageboy II in the 1970s, did not initially incorporate haptic feedback. Even by late 1986, top-selling models like the Motorola Bravo still did not feature vibration capabilities [8].

Introduction of Vibration Alerts (1987–1991)

The adoption of haptic technology in pagers began in the late 1980s. In Japan, which led the world in pager technology during the 1980s, popular models such as the NTT Pocket Bell RC-101 in 1987 did not have vibration capabilities. However, by 1991, models like the Motorola Bravo Express Pager in the US began incorporating vibration alerts. This feature allowed users to receive notifications quietly without relying on auditory signals [9].

Widespread Adoption and Standardization (1991–1995)

By 1995, vibration alerts had become a standard feature in most pagers sold in the US and Japan. For instance, the Motorola Bravo Express Pager, popular in the US, as well as many Japanese models featured vibration alerts. This introduction of vibration marked a significant shift in the pager industry, setting a precedent for future personal communication devices [10, 11]. Further, this innovation was driven by not just need but also in response to social norms. In this case, a need for discreet communication methods in various environments drove this widespread adoption.

For example, the Tokyo metro has obliged its passengers to set mobile phones to silent mode, or "manner mode," since the early 2000s [12]. This rule is part of a broader effort to maintain a quiet and orderly environment on public transportation. Passengers are asked to avoid talking on the phone and keep their devices silent to minimize disturbances to others. This practice reflects Japanese societal norms that prioritize consideration for the comfort and convenience of fellow passengers.

The Decline of Pager Networks (1995–2018)

Despite the mass adoption of haptic technology in pagers, the technology faced obsolescence with the advent of more advanced personal communication devices. By 2018, the last pager networks in Japan were discontinued, signaling the end of an era for pagers. The functions once served by pagers were replaced by first-generation mobile phones, BlackBerry devices, and eventually smartphones and laptops [13].

Legacy and Influence on Future Technologies

Integrating haptic feedback in pagers set the stage for its adoption in other personal communication devices. The success of vibration alerts in pagers demonstrated the utility and user preference for tactile notifications [14], influencing subsequent innovations in mobile phones, smartphones, and laptops. The haptic feedback technology that began with pagers continues to evolve and enhance user experiences across various modern devices [15].

5.2.2   The Mobile Phone

Early Haptics (1997–1998)

In 1997, Nokia introduced the concept of a "vibrating battery" with the Nokia 3110 model. This battery, which could be swapped with a standard one, had a built-in motor that would vibrate whenever a call was received. This feature marked the mobile phone's first commercial haptic feedback [16]

First Mass-Adopted Model (1999)

The first-time haptic technology was massively adopted in a mobile phone in 1999 with the launch of the Nokia 3210. Unlike the earlier vibrating battery, the Nokia 3210 had vibration functionality built into the phone as a default feature. This model was a significant commercial success and became crucial in popularizing mobile phone haptic feedback. The adoption of vibration alerts in mobile phones followed the trend set by pagers, demonstrating an enduring user demand for silent notification methods [17].

Development Lead Time and Industry Adoption (1997–1999)

While pagers had fully adopted vibration alerts by 1995, it is worth noting that two full years passed before this feature became common in mobile phones. The Nokia

3110's vibrating battery appeared in 1997, and the Nokia 3210 with built-in vibration followed in 1999. This timeline reflects the typical development lead time cycle of 12–18 months in the mobile phone industry and of hardware products in general [2].

Evolution of Haptic Technology (2000s-Present)

Following this initial adoption, the sophistication of the haptics in mobile phones evolved significantly. In the 2000s, mobile phones transitioned from simple vibration motors to more sophisticated actuators. While the first iPhone, launched in 2007, incorporated haptic features from the start, in 2015, Apple's iPhone 6 s introduced "3D Touch," a technology that allowed the LCD screen of the phone to sense varying pressure levels and respond accordingly. Despite mixed user reviews regarding its intuitiveness, this innovation aimed to provide a high-definition tactile experience [18].

Current Trends and High-Fidelity Haptics

Today, smartphones such as Apple's iPhone and Samsung's Galaxy devices do not utilize vibration based on rotating motors with an excentric mass, but they utilize Linear Resonant Actuators (LRAs) to deliver a more precise and powerful haptic feedback [19]. This shift from Eccentric Rotating Mass (ERM) motors to LRAs has resulted in sharper and more nuanced feedback, paralleling the direction of similar incremental trends in display resolution, battery life, and data transfer speeds. The continuous improvement in haptic fidelity stems from its use for tactile feedback [20].

5.2.3 The Laptop

Introduction of Haptic Technology (2015)

The first integration of haptic technology into laptops began with Apple's launch of the first haptic-enabled laptop in 2015 [21]. This product, known as the Apple Taptic Engine, allowed the removal of the traditional clickable trackpad, replacing it with a solid glass trackpad with no moving parts. The Taptic Engine used an LRA, akin to the one used in Sony's DualShock game controllers, to simulate clicks and taps on the trackpad.

Specific Use in Laptops

Unlike mobile phones, where haptic technology is used for silent alerts and notifications, in laptops, haptic technology has been primarily used to simulate a clicking sensation [22]. This simulation has allowed for a more durable and seamless design, as the trackpad no longer contains mechanical parts that can wear out over time. Despite the innovative use of haptics in trackpads, its application has remained limited to this specific function. It has not extended to other areas, such as silent alerts or incomplete HTML form notifications.

5.3 Haptics in the Automobile Industry

The automotive industry, producing 76 million cars globally in 2023, is experiencing a significant acceleration in adopting haptic technology. In automobiles, haptics enhances both safety and the driver experience [23, 24]. It is worth noting that in automobiles, haptics is not only applied to safety systems but also to other components such as physical buttons and knobs. For example, in BMW cars, the window buttons are carefully engineered using haptic force–displacement curves to enhance the driver experience and the sense of control. However, here we will focus on safety systems.

Early Commercial Applications

One of the earliest commercialized applications of haptic technology in car safety was the Lane Keeping Assist (LKA) system. This system, which provides drivers with tactile feedback through the steering wheel, aids in maintaining lane position without cluttering visual or audio channels [25]. Since its introduction, haptic feedback systems have become increasingly common, particularly in high-end car models.

Current Use in High-End Vehicles

Today, most high-end cars feature haptic technology in their steering wheels. These systems deliver a variety of physical guidance and warnings through the steering wheel, pedals, or seat, which are robust against high-noise environments, thus promoting driver awareness and reducing response times [26–28]. For example, haptic steering guidance systems provide feedback as torque on the steering wheel during lane deviations, helping drivers stay centered and improving lane-keeping abilities while minimizing the increase in cognitive overload [29].

Advanced Feedback Mechanisms

In addition to typical "interruption"-based feedback methods (sound, light, or vibration alerts), haptics in cars operates on a "shared control" basis. Here, driver actions trigger continuous analog-response haptic feedback, enhancing the overall driving experience [30]. However, challenges such as driver inattention, false positives, and the need to accommodate individual haptic sensitivities can reduce the effectiveness of these sophisticated systems [31].

Integration in Car Dashboards

Beyond steering wheel enhancements, haptic technology is also integrated into car dashboards. Touchscreens and buttons are redesigned to incorporate haptic feedback, offering a more intuitive user experience. For instance, some features in the Mercedes-Benz S-Class reduce the need for drivers to take their eyes off the road if they want to interact with the infotainment system, promoting safer driving habits [32, 33].

Future Possibilities

Integrating haptic feedback systems in steering wheels and dashboards presents possibilities for further enhancing automotive safety features. For example, continuous advancements may include more sophisticated feedback systems seamlessly integrating with other safety and infotainment technologies, creating a more cohesive and safer driving experience [34].

5.4 Haptics in Healthcare

In minimally invasive tools, haptic feedback enhances surgical precision by allowing surgeons to sense tissue texture better and improve control during delicate procedures [35]. Haptic technology fosters improved training and education by integrating realistic feedback into medical simulators. This enables surgeons and students to practice complex procedures in a safe environment [36]. Rehabilitation programs can leverage haptics to guide patients in regaining motor skills and coordination through specific movements with haptic devices [37, 38].

Advanced prosthetics incorporate haptic technology to give amputees a more natural sense of touch and control over their artificial limbs [39]. The future holds even greater promise, with the potential for revolutionizing telemedicine through remote palpation and diagnosis and ongoing research into using haptics for remote healthcare services and chronic condition treatment [40]. For instance, [41] presented a telemedicine system that offers synchronous telemedicine consultations with the ability for direct physical examination through haptic feedback. However, challenges include developing cost-effective and user-friendly devices and navigating standardization and regulatory considerations for safe and effective integration into medical practices [42]. Further exploration is recommended into specific applications like surgical robotics [43], rehabilitation therapy [44], and prosthetic development [45] while also considering the ethical implications of haptics in healthcare, such as potential data privacy concerns [46].

5.5 Haptics in Aviation and Military

Haptic technology is being increasingly adopted via innovative applications in the aviation and military sectors. In aviation, haptic feedback can enhance pilot training by equipping flight simulators with a more realistic feel of aircraft controls during various scenarios, potentially improving pilot proficiency and decision-making in critical situations [47, 48]. Haptics can also be integrated into aircraft maintenance and inspection tools. This integration provides technicians with tactile feedback while examining surfaces for potential anomalies or damage, leading to earlier detection [34].

The military sector sees similar potential, with haptic feedback incorporated into joysticks and control systems for military vehicles and weapons, offering soldiers a more intuitive feel and precise control over weapon systems [35]. Furthermore, haptic vests or gloves could communicate tactical information on the battlefield through subtle vibrations, reducing reliance on visual displays and potentially improving situational awareness [36]. For instance, Ozioko et al. [49] presented smart gloves integrating gesture and touch functionalities, serving military applications like tele-manipulation, training, and virtual collaboration. Teleoperation and remote manipulation are other areas where haptics can play a crucial role, allowing soldiers to remotely control robots or drones with a more natural sense of touch and feedback [37]. For instance, [50] presented a device that enhances teleoperation and precision in military and robotic applications by providing force and surface information feedback. This application enables users to remotely control robots or drones with greater accuracy and tactile feedback.

The future holds promise for revolutionizing pilot training through highly realistic haptic simulation experiences, and integration with augmented reality displays could further enhance situational awareness and decision-making in aviation and military settings. However, current challenges in applying haptics in these two fields include developing robust and reliable haptic systems for demanding environments and carefully considering standardization and safety regulations for safe and effective integration [38]. Further exploration is recommended into specific advancements in haptic flight simulators, the use of haptics in robotic control systems for military applications, and the potential human factors and safety implications of this technology in these critical fields [51].

5.6   Gap Matrix Analysis

Table 5.1 provides a qualitative gap matrix [52] that indicates the prevalence of haptic technology use across different application areas. This matrix offers a qualitative assessment of adopting and implementing various haptic technology features in diverse product categories. The values in the matrix are based on our observations and serve as qualitative suggestions.

Purpose and Utility

Gap matrices are employed to identify emerging niches that have the potential to become significant research or commercial hotspots. As discussed in the foresight section of the introduction and the pager case study, the know-how of automobile analogic force feedback can be transferred to other verticals with similar user needs, such as noisy environments that require safety improvements. This matrix, although qualitative, can be a valuable tool for researchers and planners to identify potential technology transfer opportunities and assess functionality while pointing toward future opportunities.

Table 5.1 Gap matrix analysis

Product/vertical	Feature				
	Silent alert	Emulate physical buttons	Bone-to-ear audio	Air gestures	Analogic force feedback
High-end automobile (lane departure, lane assist)	100%	–	–	–	100%
Motorcycles	–	–	–	–	–
Smartphone	100%	–	–	–	–
Laptop trackpad	–	Low	–	–	–
Keyboard		–	–	–	–
Wearable watch	100%	Low	–	Experimental*	–
VR/AR headset	–	–	Low	–	–
Healthcare devices	–	–	–	–	–
Factory safety	–	–	–	–	–

Note * See wrist gestures in Wear OS by Google

5.7 Applying Foresight to Forecast Haptic Trends

Foresight is a strategic planning methodology that allows organizations to anticipate future trends and challenges. The practice enables them to make informed decisions that shape desirable outcomes. It is not about predicting the future but rather exploring and preparing for multiple possible futures. This section frames our analysis and recommendations on haptics technology adoption across various industries.

Applying Foresight Methodologies

Foresight methodologies include a range of techniques such as horizon scanning, scenario planning, backcasting, and causal layered analysis. These methods help identify emerging trends, explore future possibilities, and develop strategic responses. By leveraging these techniques, we can better understand how haptics technology might evolve and impact a range of sectors.

1. *Horizon Scanning*: Horizon scanning involves systematically exploring the external environment to identify potential opportunities and threats. For instance, in the context of haptics, we can scan for advancements in related technologies such as artificial intelligence, virtual reality (VR), and wearable devices. This can help us identify how these technologies might integrate with or enhance haptic feedback systems. For example, through our gap matrix analysis, we can see that more and more moving parts are being replaced by haptic keyboards (Blackberry, trackpad in Apple laptops). The insight leads us to speculate which other physical buttons could be replaced.

2. *Scenario Planning*: Scenario planning involves creating detailed and plausible scenarios of the future based on different assumptions. For example, we could develop scenarios in which haptic technology becomes ubiquitous in consumer electronics versus scenarios in which its adoption is limited to specific niche markets. This helps organizations prepare for various outcomes and devise flexible strategies [53].
3. *Backcasting*: Backcasting starts with defining a desirable future and then working backward to identify the steps needed to achieve that future. In the case of haptics, we envision a future where haptic feedback is a standard feature in all automotive safety systems. We would then identify the technological, regulatory, and market developments necessary to reach this state.
4. *Causal Layered Analysis (CLA)*: CLA is a popular choice to explore the underlying causes and worldviews that shape current and future trends. Applying CLA to haptics in automotive industries, we can explore the technological factors and the cultural, social, and economic drivers influencing adoption. This holistic view helps in creating more robust strategies.

Strategic Recommendations for Haptics Technology

1. **Enhancing User Experience**: A way to enhance user experience is to integrate haptics into user interfaces across different devices by (i) refining the tactile feedback and (ii) standardizing haptic patterns and other actions in smartphones. An example of how standardization helped adoption can be found in the case study of the cassette tape standard by Philips [54].
2. **Safety Applications in the Automotive Industry**: Haptics technology has significant potential to improve automotive safety. The current trend indicates that the automotive industry is leading in analogic feedback. This leadership—in terms of both product and cost—could be translated to the medical verticals with unfavorable trade-offs that prevent wider adoption of haptics.
3. **Cross-Industry Technology Transfer**: As mentioned, the principles and technologies developed for haptics in one industry can often be adapted for use in another. For example, advancements in haptic feedback systems in gaming can be transferred to medical simulations or remote robotic surgery. Cross-industry partnerships and research initiatives can facilitate this technology transfer and drive innovation. The case of LRA, where Apple followed Sony's lead in adopting LRA, illustrates the usefulness of said transfers.

5.8 Intellectual Patents on Haptics

This section discusses patents in healthcare, gaming, and automobiles. It outlines how advancement in haptic device patents has evolved from initial use to the present.

5.8.1 Patents in Healthcare

Table 5.2 summarizes haptic-based patents in healthcare. These patents cover a range of applications. For instance, a robotic surgery training system [55] uses force feedback to guide pupils' movements, while an intraoperative planning tool [56] employs haptic objects to guide surgeons and avoid anatomical obstacles. Surgical instruments [57] provide tactile feedback for tissue manipulation and a haptic user interface [58] precisely controls robotic surgical tools.

Table 5.2 Examples of haptic-related patents in healthcare

Reference	Device	Feedback type	Application
Wang et al. [55]	Minimally invasive surgical training using robotics and telecollaboration	Force	To train via a robotic surgery system with force feedback for effective teaching
Abovitz et al. [56]	System and method for intraoperative haptic planning of a medical procedure	Force and vibration	To guide surgeons to target areas and avoid obstacles
Ramsay et al. [59]	Haptic health feedback monitoring	Force and vibration	To monitor health parameters and alert users with specific haptic feedback
Karkanias and Hodges [61]	Haptic support and virtual activity monitor	Force	To monitor motion and provide haptic feedback for rehabilitation
Morbi et al. [60]	Control system and device for patient assistance	Force	To control haptic and motorized patient assist devices using stability boundaries
Yoo et al. [62]	Vibrating haptic device for the blind	Vibration	To combine vibrating haptic device and mobile device for navigation
Shelton et al. [57]	Controlling a surgical instrument according to sensed closure parameters	Force and vibration	To detect tissue compression and provide tactile feedback during surgery
Schnur et al. [58]	Haptic user interface for robotically controlled surgical instruments	Force	To provide a user interface for precise control of robotic surgical instruments
Assi et al. [63]	A user interface and system for supplying gases to an airway	Vibration	To provide wearable respiratory support with haptic feedback for gas flow adjustment

Haptic patents are also used for monitoring and alerts. For example, health feedback monitors [59] use parametric sensors to alert users with specific haptic feedback based on physiological parameters. Similarly, patient assistance devices [60] utilize sensors and actuators for stability and control. A virtual activity monitor [61] helps with rehabilitation by motion monitoring and haptic feedback. For navigation aids, a vibrating haptic device for the visually impaired [62] combines tactile feedback with positioning sensors to aid in user orientation. Lastly, a respiratory support device [63] integrates haptic feedback to optimize gas flow adjustment, enhancing user interaction and safety.

5.8.2 Patents in Gaming and Entertainment

Table 5.3 shows some haptic-related patents in gaming and entertainment. Interactive gaming systems like those by [64, 65] use handheld controllers with sensors to detect movements, providing haptic feedback for actions like hitting a ball and focused vibrations to make buttons and joysticks more realistic. Similarly, [66] created a customizable tactile feedback method integrated into gaming devices through touch-sensitive interfaces.

In 3-D gaming, [67] developed a haptic stylus that simulates tactile sensations and friction forces on touch screens, while [68] patented a method allowing users to interact with virtual objects using gestures and a stylus, delivering tactile feedback through physical overlays and haptic interfaces.

For accessibility, [69] developed a refreshable braille display accessory for game controllers, providing dynamic tactile braille feedback for visually impaired players. Khurana [70] improved gameplay with tactile and auditory cues, enhancing engagement and accessibility through haptic feedback. Seiler [71] integrated drone vibrations into a VR vest, allowing users to feel synchronized drone movements, adding a new dimension to VR experiences. Finally, [72] developed a touch-sensitive keypad to ensure precise haptic feedback while maintaining an interactive surface.

5.8.3 Patents in the Automobile Industry

Our search for haptic patents in automobiles revealed many innovative uses. These patents focus on driver comfort, control, awareness, and safety applications, as shown in Table 5.4.

For driver comfort and control, [73] presented a haptic feedback system for vehicle seating that enhances comfort by providing customizable seat vibrations and reducing driver fatigue. Similarly, [74] introduced a gesture-based input system with haptic feedback, enabling intuitive control of vehicle systems through gesture recognition to improve user interaction and safety. Provancher [75] developed a shear tactile display system that provides precise three-dimensional feedback for control inputs,

Table 5.3 Examples of haptic-related patents in gaming and entertainment

References	Device	Feedback-type	Application
Strawn et al. [72]	Touch-sensitive keypad with tactile feedback	Vibration	To harness touch sensors and biased switches for precise haptic feedback on key presses
Adhikari [67]	Haptic device for 3-D gaming	Vibration	To simulate tactile sensations and friction on touch screens
Endo and Jasso [64]	Interactive gaming systems with haptic feedback	Vibration	To detect movements, providing haptic feedback for immersion via a handheld device
Grant [65]	Gaming device with haptic effect isolated to user input elements	Vibration and force	To provide realistic sensory feedback with focused vibrations
Tran et al. [69]	Refreshable braille display accessory for a game controller	Vibration	To provide a refreshable braille display for game controllers, updating with in-game text/audio
Seiler [71]	VR system with drone integration	Vibration and force	To provide a VR vest with tactile vibration from a synchronized drone
Mahlmeister et al. [66]	Gaming accessory with sensory feedback device	Vibration	To give customizable tactile feedback in gaming devices through touch interfaces
Pahud et al. [68]	Hover-based user interactions with virtual objects within immersive environments	Vibration	To allow gestures and stylus interactions with tactile feedback for virtual objects
Khurana [70]	Tactile and audio-enabled gaming	Vibration	To provide tactile and auditory cues to enhance the gaming experience and accessibility

particularly for steering, enhancing driver awareness. Brown et al. [76] proposed a haptic driving guidance system that assists drivers with vehicle controls, offering tactile cues for adjustments like gear selection, steering, acceleration, and braking. Chung et al. [77] presented a remote-control unit with active feedback, ensuring smooth transitions between remote and autonomous modes in vehicle control by reflecting the vehicle's operational status through tactile cues.

Table 5.4 Examples of haptic-related patents in automobiles

References	Device	Feedback-type	Application
Veen and Jarocha [73]	The haptic feedback system for vehicle seating	Vibration	Customizable seat vibrations for comfort and reduced fatigue
Truong [74]	Gesture-based input system in a vehicle with haptic feedback	Vibration	Gesture-based control with tactile feedback for safety
Yamashita et al. [81]	Touch panel vehicle information display device	Vibration	Touch panel with tactile feedback for better usability
Modarres et al. [78]	Systems and methods for awareness in vehicles using haptic effects	Vibration and force	Tactile seat belt alerts for environmental or vehicle conditions
Provancher [75]	Shear tactile display system for communicating direction and other tactile cues	Vibration and tactile	A finger thimble providing 3D feedback for steering control
Hakim and Khaled [79]	System and method for sound direction detection in a vehicle	Vibration	Haptic feedback on the steering wheel for sound direction
Giraud and Kwong [80]	Haptically-enabled motorcycles	Vibration	Haptic alerts on motorcycle handlebars, footpegs, and seat
Bernardo et al. [82]	Haptic and thermal feedback touchpad device, system, and method for an automotive setting	Thermal and vibration	Tactile and thermal feedback for driver safety and guidance
Brown et al. [76]	Haptic driving guidance system	Force and vibration	Tactile cues for adjusting vehicle controls without visual input
Chung et al. [77]	Remote control unit having active feedback	Force	Haptic feedback for transitioning between remote and autonomous modes

Regarding driver awareness and safety, [78] integrated haptic feedback into seat belts, providing tactile alerts based on environmental or vehicle conditions. Hakim and Khaled [79] enhanced driver awareness of significant sounds, such as sirens or honking, using haptic feedback on the steering wheel to provide directional cues. Giraud and Kwong [80] designed haptically enabled motorcycles with devices on handlebars, footpegs, and seats that alert riders to hazards, enhancing rider safety.

For touch and interaction, [81] presented a touch panel vehicle information display that provides tactile feedback, improving usability during vehicle operation. Bernardo et al. [82] presented a haptic and thermal feedback touchpad device for automotive settings, integrating tactile and thermal feedback to enhance driver awareness and safety by analyzing vehicle operation data and providing guiding sensations.

5.9 Conclusion

In summary, haptic technology has diffused [83] over the years, from pagers to other sectors and verticals. Haptic devices are today utilized across various fields, including healthcare and gaming, offering better user experiences and safety features. Except for the case of laptops (where adoption seems stalled), we found no evidence that adoption will pause, revert, or stop.

The chapter introduced how to use gap matrix tools for future planning and foresight, showing how common haptics is in various applications. This analysis might help identify new areas for research or commercial growth.

The chapter also covered intellectual patent trends across healthcare, gaming, and automobiles. In healthcare, haptic technology helps improve surgical precision, patient monitoring, and aids for the visually impaired. In gaming and entertainment, patents claim that haptic feedback can improve user interaction, immersion, and accessibility to make experiences realistic and engaging.

In the automotive industry, patents claim to improve driver comfort, sense of control, and safety, mainly through innovations in seating, gesture control, and tactile alerts.

Acknowledgements This research was funded by the joint UAEU-ZU grant no. R22021, and Joana Lepore for advice on foresight.

References

1. Precedence Research: Haptic Technology Market (2023). https://www.precedenceresearch. com/haptic-technology-market
2. Oh, J., Yoon, S.-J.: Validation of haptic enabling technology acceptance model (HE-TAM): integration of IDT and TAM. Telemat. Inform. **31**(4), 585–596 (2014)
3. Kapoor, S., et al.: Haptics: touchfeedback technology widening the horizon of medicine. J. Clin. Diagn. Res. JCDR **8**(3), 294–299 (2014)
4. Enayati, N., De Momi, E., Ferrigno, G.: Haptics in robot-assisted surgery: challenges and benefits. IEEE Rev. Biomed. Eng. **9**, 49–65 (2016)
5. Barbash, G.I., Glied, S.A.: New technology and health care costs: the case of robot-assisted surgery. New Engl. J. Med. **363**, 701–704 (2010)
6. Guo, Z., Zhang, Y., Hu, Q.: Integrated vibration isolation and attitude control for spacecraft with uncertain or unknown payload inertia parameters. Acta Astron. **151**, 107–119 (2018)

7. Wikipedia: Market Share of Personal Computer Vendors (2023). https://en.wikipedia.org/wiki/Market_share_of_personal_computer_vendors

8. Strobel, R.A.: Operation Bandit-CIM from a user perspective. In: Proceedings of the 15th Annual Conference of IEEE Industrial Electronics Society (1989)

9. Polyplastics: Pocket Bell with Display (2008). https://www.polyplastics.com/en/pavilion/doc omo/1987.html. Accessed 10 May 2024

10. Motorola: Motorola Milestones (2018). https://www.motorola.com/us/about/motorola-his tory-milestones

11. Verhoef, J.: The Rise of Chronic Reachability and the Accelerated, Flexible Society: The Social Construction of the Pager, 1987–1999. Mobile Media and Communication (2023)

12. Padoan, T.: Drawn by images: control, subversion and contamination in the visual discourse of Tokyo Metro. Lexia J. Semiot. **32**, 579–599 (2014)

13. phys.org: Turning the Page: Japan's Last Pager Service Ends After 50 Years (2018). https://phys.org/news/2018-12-page-japan-pager-years.html

14. Roumen, T., Perrault, S.T., Zhao, S.: NotiRing: a comparative study of notification channels for wearable interactive rings. In: Proceedings of the 33rd Annual ACM Conference on Human Factors in Computing Systems (CHI'15) (2015)

15. Goodman, B.: I hear ringing and there's no one there i wonder why (2016). https://www.nyt imes.com/2006/05/04/fashion/thursdaystyles/04phan.html. Accessed 6 May 2024

16. Varshavskii, A.E., Kuznetsova, M.S.: Analyzing the indicators of innovative development of smartphones (the case of Nokia smartphones produced by Nokia, Microsoft, and HMD). Natl. Interests Priorit. Sec. **12**(417), 2379–2405 (2022)

17. LPCwiki: Nokia 3210 (2024). https://lpcwiki.miraheze.org/wiki/Nokia_3210. Accessed 11 May 2024

18. Park, J., Nam, C., Lee, J., Shin, D.: Analysis of Task Success Rate for Classifying 2D-Touch and 3D-Touch through Threshold, pp. 334–338 (2019)

19. Pyo, D., Yang, T., Ryu, S., Kwon, D.: Novel linear impact-resonant actuator for mobile applications. Sens. Actuat. A Phys. **65**, 460–471 (2015)

20. Wang, Y.-W., et al.: Demonstration of JetController: High-speed Ungrounded Force Feedback Controllers Using Air Propulsion Jets. Association for Computing Machinery, New York (2021)

21. Gibbs, S.: Apple's 'force touch' and 'taptic engine' explained. Guardian **11**, 3 (2015)

22. Boreas: Why Haptic Trackpads Are More Than A Trend (2022). https://pages.boreas.ca/blog/piezo-haptics/haptic-trackpads-are-more-than-just-a-trend. Accessed 24 May 2024

23. Acea: Economic and Market Report: Global and EU Auto Industry—Full Year 2023 (2024). https://www.acea.auto/publication/economic-and-market-report-global-and-eu-auto-industry-full-year-2023/

24. Sun, X. & Zhao, Y., 2023. Application of haptic feedback technology in automotive information systems. Huanan. Ligong. Daxue. Xuebao J. South China Univ. Technol. 51(8), pp. 98 - 109.

25. Roozendaal, J., et al.: Haptic lane-keeping assistance for truck driving: a test track study. Hum. Fact. **63**(8), 1380–1395 (2021)

26. Balachandran, A., Brown, M., Erlien, S., Gerdes, J.: Predictive haptic feedback for obstacle avoidance based on model predictive control. IEEE Trans. Autom. Sci. Eng. **13**, 26–31 (2016)

27. Jensen, M., et al.: A customizable automotive steering system with a haptic feedback control strategy for obstacle avoidance notification. IEEE Trans. Vehic. Technol. **60**, 4208–4216 (2011)

28. Telpaz, A., Rhindress, B., Zelman, I., Tsimhoni, O.: Haptic Seat for Automated Driving: Preparing the Driver to Take Control Effectively (2015)

29. Wang, Z., et al.: The effect of a haptic guidance steering system on fatigue-related driver behavior. IEEE Trans. Hum. Mach. Syst. **47**(5), 741–748 (2017)

30. Boink, R., Van Paassen, M.M., Mulder, M., Abbink, D.A.: Understanding and reducing conflicts between driver and haptic shared control. In: Conference Proceedings—IEEE International Conference on Systems, Man and Cybernetics (2014)

31. Richter, H., Ecker, R., Deisler, C., Butz, A.: HapTouch and the 2+1 State Model: Potentials of Haptic Feedback on Touch Based in-Vehicle Information Systems (2010)
32. Mercedes-Benz: Mercedes-Benz of Arrowhead (2023). https://www.arrowheadmb.com/. Accessed 11 May 2024
33. Tivadar, R.I., et al.: Digital haptics improve speed of visual search performance in a dual-task setting. Sci. Rep. **12**(1), 98 (2022)
34. Lu, M., Wevers, K., Heijden, R.: Technical feasibility of advanced driver assistance systems (ADAS) for road traffic safety. Transp. Plann. Technol. **28**, 167–187 (2005)
35. Puangmali, P., et al.: State-of-the-art in force and tactile sensing for minimally invasive surgery. IEEE Sens. J. **8**, 371–381 (2008)
36. Basdogan, C., et al.: Haptics in minimally invasive surgical simulation and training. IEEE Comput. Graph. Appl. **32**, 56–64 (2004)
37. Broeren, J., Rydmark, M., Sunnerhagen, K.: Virtual reality and haptics as a training device for movement rehabilitation after stroke: a single-case study. Arch. Phys. Med. Rehabil. **85**(8), 1247–1250 (2004)
38. Kim, H., Lee, M., Kim, J.: Effects of additional haptic feedback during mirror therapy for upper limb motor recovery in stroke patients: a pilot randomized controlled trial. J. Stroke Cerebrovasc. Dis. **31**(2), 9856 (2022)
39. Kim, K., Colgate, J.: Haptic feedback enhances grip force control of sEMG-controlled prosthetic hands in targeted reinnervation amputees. IEEE Trans. Neural Syst. Rehabil. Eng. **20**, 798–805 (2012)
40. Cascella, M., et al.: Open issues and practical suggestions for telemedicine in chronic pain. Int. J. Environ. Res. Public Health **18**, 8758 (2021)
41. Husman, M., et al.: A Wearable Skin Stretch Haptic Feedback Device: Towards Improving Balance Control in Lower Limb Amputees, pp. 2120–2123. IEEE (2016)
42. Khatri, N., Kumar, M., Jha, R.: Opportunities and challenges in medical robotic device development. Mater. Horizons Nat. Nanomater. **32**, 299–313 (2022)
43. Amirabdollahian, F., et al.: Prevalence of haptic feedback in robot-mediated surgery: a systematic review of literature. J. Robot. Surg. **12**(1), 11–25 (2018)
44. Hani, J.B., et al.: Users' Perspectives on Haptic Technology Use in Hand Rehabilitation. In: ACM International Conference Proceeding Series (2021)
45. Dey, A., Basumatary, H., Hazarika, S.M.: A decade of haptic feedback for upper limb prostheses. IEEE Trans. Med. Robot. Bion. **5**(4), 793–810 (2023)
46. Gavette, H., et al.: Advances in prosthetic technology: a perspective on ethical considerations for development and clinical translation. Front. Rehabil. Sci. **4**, 985 (2024)
47. Van Baelen, D., et al.: Evaluating Stick Stiffness and Position Guidance for Feedback on Flight Envelope Protection. Virtual, AIAA Scitech 2021 Forum (2021)
48. Zikmund, P., Horpatzka, M., Macik, M.: Learning effect in joystick tactile guidance. IEEE Trans. Hapt. **32**, 1–11 (2024)
49. Ozioko, O., Dahiya, R.: Smart tactile gloves for haptic interaction, communication, and rehabilitation. Adv. Intell. Syst. **4**(2), 392–413 (2021)
50. Dede, M., Selvi, Ö., Bilgincan, T., Kant, Y.: Design of a Haptic Device for Teleoperation and Virtual Reality Systems. IEEE (2009)
51. Xavier, R., Silva, J.L., Ventura, R.: Pseudo-haptics interfaces for robotic teleoperation. In: ACM/IEEE International Conference on Human-Robot Interaction (2024)
52. Berengueres, J., Sandell, M.: Introduction to Data Visualization and Storytelling (2019)
53. Canyon, D.: Simplifying complexity with strategic foresight and scenario planning. Sec. Nexus **22**, 54–63 (2021)
54. Johnson, M.: Competitive dynamics in the audio industry. Int. J. Ind. Organ. **6**(2), 215–234 (1988)
55. Wang, Y., et al.: Minimally Invasive Surgical Training Using Robotics and Telecollaboration. USA, Patent No. US6852107B2 (2005)
56. Abovitz, R.A., Quaid, A.E.I., Santos-Munne, J.J.: System and Method for Intra-Operative Haptic Planning of a Medical Procedure. USA, Patent No. US7206627B2 (2007)

57. Shelton, F.E.I., et al.: Controlling a Surgical Instrument According to Sensed Closure Parameters. USA, Patent No. US20190201018A1 (2020)
58. Schnur, P.W., Atay, S., Hufford, K.A., Penny, M.R.: Haptic User Interface for Robotically Controlled Surgical Instruments. USA, Patent No. US11540890B2 (2023)
59. Ramsay, E., Heubel, R., Olien, N.: Haptic Health Feedback Monitoring. Patent No. WO2009002577A1 (2008)
60. Morbi, A., Ahmadi, M., Beranek, R.: Control System and Device for Patient Assist. Patent No. CA2867484C (2018)
61. Karkanias, C., Hodges, S.: Haptic Support and Virtual Activity Monitor. USA, Patent No. US7993291B2 (2011)
62. Yoo, K., Kirkland, K., Wang, Y.: Vibrating Haptic Device for the Blind. USA, Patent No. US10371544B2 (2019)
63. Assi, M.S., et al.: A User Interface and System for Supplying Gases to an Airway. Patent No. AU2021232661B2 (2023)
64. Endo, S., Jasso, S.: Interactive Gaming Systems with Haptic Feedback. USA, Patent No. US8992322B2 (2015)
65. Grant, D.: Gaming Device with Haptic Effect Isolated to User Input Elements. Korea, Patent No. KR20150054670 (2015)
66. Mahlmeister, J.N., et al.: Gaming Accessory with Sensory Feedback Device. USA, Patent No. US10898799B2 (2021)
67. Adhikari, S.: Haptic Device for 3-D Gaming. USA, Patent No. US8956230B2 (2015)
68. Pahud, M., et al.: Hover-Based User-Interactions with Virtual Objects Within Immersive Environments. USA, Patent No. US11068111B2 (2021)
69. Tran, J., et al.: Refreshable Braille Display Accessory for a Game Controller. USA, Patent No. US10463978B2 (2018)
70. Khurana, R.: Tactile and Audio-Enabled Gaming. USA, Patent No. US11235229B1 (2022)
71. Seiler, B.: Virtual Reality System with Drone Integration. USA, Patent No. US10535195B2 (2020)
72. Strawn, A., et al.: Touch Sensitive Keypad with Tactile Feedback. USA, Patent No. US8139035B2 (2012)
73. Veen, G., Jarocha, W.: Haptic Feedback System for Vehicle Seating. USA, Patent No. US8942892B2 (2015)
74. Truong, D.: Gesture Based Input System in a Vehicle with Haptic Feedback. USA, Patent No. US9248840B2 (2016)
75. Provancher, W.: Shear Tactile Display System for Communicating Direction and Other Tactile Cues. Europe, Patent No. EP2183660B1 (2019)
76. Brown, A., Fibich, J., Mati, S., Disenso, D.: Haptic Driving Guidance System. China, Patent No. CN109475079B (2023)
77. Chung, S., Peters, R., Louis, A.: Remote Control Unit Having Active Feedback. USA, Patent No. US11543819B2 (2023)
78. Modarres, A., Cruz-Hernandez, J.M., Grant, D.A., Olien, N.: Systems and Methods for Awareness in Vehicles Using Haptic Effects. USA, Patent No. US10232773B2 (2019)
79. Hakim, M., Khaled, O.: System and Method for Sound Direction Detection in a Vehicle. China, Patent No. CN107852179B (2020)
80. Giraud, D., Kwong, D.: Haptically Enabled Motorcycle. USA, Patent No. US10926780B2 (2021)
81. Yamashita, K., Kamiyama, H., Imai, C.: Touch Panel Vehicle Information Display Device. Japan, Patent No. JP6315456B2 (2018)
82. Bernardo, P., et al.: Haptic and Thermal Feedback Touchpad Device, System and Method Thereof for an Automotive Setting. Patent No. WO2023126660A1 (2023)
83. Geroski, P.A.: Models of technology diffusion. Res. Policy **4–5**(29), 603–625 (2000)
84. Alexiou, J.E.A.: Multistage Tactile Sound Device. USA, Patent No. US20150063606A1 (2017)

85. Barrera, O., Sartor, J.: Haptic Feedback Device for Surgical Instruments and Robotic Surgical Systems. USA, Patent No. US20220000573A1 (2022)

86. Bian, Y., et al.: An advanced lane-keeping assistance system with switchable assistance modes. IEEE Trans. Intell. Transp. Syst. **21**, 385–396 (2020)

87. Breitschaft, S.J., Clarke, S., Carbon, C.-C.: A theoretical framework of haptic processing in automotive user interfaces and its implications on design and engineering. Front. Psychol. **10**, 5423 (2019)

88. BusinessWeek: Motorola's Pageboy II: Tripling the Market. BusinessWeek, pp. 53-4 (1973)

89. Chauvelin, C., Sagi, T.: Characterization of generic and personalized on-screen vibrotactile patterns. In: Proceedings of the 2014 6th International Conference on Intelligent Human-Machine Systems and Cybernetics, IHMSC 2014 (2014)

90. Cunningham, R.E.A.: Haptic Interface for Palpation Simulation. USA, Patent No. US7307619B2 (2007)

91. Duke, W.: Tactile Sudoku Game Display for the Blind. USA, Patent No. US20100311019A1 (2010)

92. Erp, J., Veen, H.: Vibro-Tactile Information Presentation in Automobiles. Birmingham (2001)

93. Gaffary, Y., Lécuyer, A.: The use of haptic and tactile information in the car to improve driving safety: a review of current technologies. Front. ICT **5**(3), 64 (2018)

94. González-Cañete, F., López-Rodríguez, J., Galdón, P., Diaz-Estrella, S.: Improving the screen exploration of smartphones using haptic icons for visually impaired users. Sensors **21**(15), 1154 (2021)

95. Gordon, M.L., Zhai, S.: Touchscreen haptic augmentation effects on tapping, drag and drop, and path following. In: The 2019 CHI Conference on Human Factors in Computing Systems (CHI '19) (2019)

96. Hamza-Lup, F.G., Goldbach, I.R.: Multimodal, visuo-haptic games for abstract theory instruction: grabbing charged particles. J. Multimodal User Interf. **15**(1), 5985 (2021)

97. Jeong, S., Yun, H.H., Lee, Y., Han, Y.: Glow the buzz: a VR puzzle adventure game mainly played through haptic feedback. In: Conference on Human Factors in Computing Systems—Proceedings (2023)

98. Kim, H.-Y., Kim, J.: A study of implementation of kinesthetic feedback on game framework using the haptic device for realistic interaction. Int. J. Appl. Eng. Res. **10**(10), 27205–27212 (2015)

99. Komura, M., Hagihira, T., Ogasawara, M.: New radio paging system and its propagation characteristics. IEEE Trans. Vehic. Technol. **26**(4), 362–366 (1977)

100. Kumar, L.V.M.: Touch and explore: a VR game exploration, based on haptic driven game-play. In: Virtual, ISS 2021 of the Companion Proceedings of the 2021 Conference on Interactive Surfaces and Spaces (2021)

101. Lehman, S.: The Mysteries of Japan-Only Phones (2020). https://sabukaru.online/articles/the-mysterious-early-world-of-japans-cellphone-culture

102. McNew, J.-M., Prokhorov, D., Toyoda, H.: Vehicular Haptic Feedback System and Method. USA, Patent No. US9827811B1 (2017)

103. Myers, S., Rigazio, L.: Versatile Keyboard Input and Output Device. USA, Patent No. US20160004329A1 (2016)

104. Peruvemba, S.: Please, touch the display. Solid State Technol. **60**(2), 10–11 (2017)

105. Poupyrev, I., Maruyama, S.: Tactile interfaces for small touch screens. In: Proceedings of the 16th Annual ACM Symposium on User Interface Software and Technology (UIST '03) (2003)

106. Pryor, T.: Programmable Tactile Touch Screen Displays and Man-Machine Interfaces for Improved Vehicle Instrumentation and Telematics. USA, Patent No. US20090322499A1 (2009)

107. Retroist: The Bellboy and the History of Telephone Pagers (2023). https://www.retroist.com/p/the-bellboy-and-the-history-of-telephone

108. Rosenberg, L., Braun, A., Levin, M.: Method and apparatus for controlling force feedback interface utilizing host computer. Japan, Patent No. JP2010061667A (2010)

109. Shi, G.E.A.: Fluidic haptic interface for mechano-tactile feedback. IEEE Trans. Hapt. **13**(1), 204–210 (2020)
110. UK Radio History: Radio History UK (2021). https://radiohistory.uk/. Accessed 18 June 2024
111. Wikipedia: Nokia 3110 (2024). https://en.wikipedia.org/wiki/Nokia_3110. Accessed 11 May 2024

Chapter 6
Conclusions and Final Remarks

Abstract This chapter ties together the haptics topics explored throughout the book. It aims to provide an understanding of the essential ideas presented in the book by summarizing and synthesizing the key takeaways from the previous chapters. Finally, the chapter also offers final remarks to conclude the book.

Keywords Haptics · Overview

6.1 Conclusions

6.1.1 Chapter 1: Introduction to Haptic Technology

Chapter 1 has defined *haptic technology* as the creation of the sense of touch in digital environments using forces, vibrations, or motions. This technology integrates principles from various fields, including engineering, computer science, and human perception. Haptic-based feedback systems interact with slow and fast-adapting receptors in the skin to convey information through texture, force, and pressure.

Hence, haptic technology uses various principles to deliver such feedback to the skin. These include force, pressure, vibrations, thermal, and airflow. Additionally, the feedback can be delivered by stimulating the human nerves and muscles, bypassing the receptors.

Force feedback occurs when haptic devices apply mechanical simulation felt by the human kinesthetic system. By delivering reaction forces, force feedback can be useful in aiding the visually impaired and enhancing VR interactions and telesurgeries.

Vibration feedback uses vibrations to simulate touch sensations. This type of feedback enhances user experience and performance in various interactive tasks. In VR, vibrations provide collision emulation, improving immersion and interaction. In physical therapy and motor learning, vibration aids in learning new motor skills, reduces errors, and improves the learning curve, especially in arm motion training.

M. A. Kuhail et al., *Advances, Applications and the Future of Haptic Technology*,
SpringerBriefs in Computer Science, https://doi.org/10.1007/978-3-031-70588-5_6

Thermal feedback devices create heat or cold sensations, which creates a more realistic experience. This type of feedback can assist visually impaired individuals and offer potential therapeutic uses for brain stimulation in dementia or coma patients. *Airflow feedback* uses air jets for a nonintrusive interaction, enhancing realism in virtual environments with simulated air movements.

Transcutaneous electrical nerve stimulation (TENS) uses electrical currents to stimulate nerve endings. It bypasses the stimulation of the body's touch receptors and instead stimulates the nerves directly, offering a potential avenue to thinner and slimmer haptic devices that are currently experimental.

Haptic feedback can also be categorized by how users interact. *Wearable haptics*, like gloves or vests, provide touch feedback directly on the body. *Touchable haptics* are surfaces you interact with, like touchscreens that vibrate when you press them. Finally, *graspable haptics* are virtual objects you can hold and feel their texture and shape.

Haptic technology advancements are driven by three main factors: improving user experience (think realistic gaming experiences), military needs (like better robot control), and understanding human touch (how we perceive different sensations).

6.1.2 Chapter 2: Exploring the Role of Haptic Technology in Healthcare

Chapter 2 provided an overview of haptic technology in healthcare. Haptics have been integrated into medical training and surgery simulations. For example, medical training is enhanced by devices like CyberGlove capture hand movements and provide tactile feedback, enhancing medical training even during COVID-19 restrictions.

The chapter highlighted the benefits of vibrotactile feedback for individuals with sensory deficits, enhancing mobility and safety. Meanwhile, force feedback is used in shoes to augment the sense of virtual terrains for rehabilitation. TENS restores sensory feedback in amputees and aids muscle relaxation, while the Teslasuit uses it for exercise correction.

Wearable haptic devices like LinkTouch, hRing, and TacTiles have found applications in medical surgery and therapy. For example, LinkTouch provides precise force feedback at the fingertips, enabling surgeons to practice delicate procedures with realistic tissue resistance and manipulation sensations. hRing's ability to stretch the skin to emulate touch or grip sensations is beneficial for patients recovering from hand injuries or surgeries. TacTiles can provide localized pressure points that mimic the sensation of different textures and surfaces. This is useful in sensory re-education therapy for patients with nerve damage or neurological conditions, helping them regain sensory perception and tactile discrimination.

Haptic technology is also used in dental, brain, maxillofacial, and amputation surgeries by providing realistic tactile feedback, which is crucial for developing fine motor skills. Additionally, it is used in knee surgery simulations and gait support, improving surgical accuracy and patient rehabilitation. Haptic systems in smart insoles and rehabilitation tools provide real-time feedback, aiding in safe walking and reducing cognitive load.

6.1.3 Chapter 3: Exploring Haptic Technology in Gaming and Entertainment

Chapter 3 has shown how haptic technology is integrated into gaming, adding a new dimension of realism and engagement beyond traditional visuals and sounds. The emergent uses of haptic devices have found innovative uses in serious games. Surgeons can train for delicate suturing procedures using haptic feedback that simulates the sensation of applying force with needles and thread. Additionally, physicians use haptic-based games like Whack-a-Mole to create interactive rehabilitation exercises for upper limbs. Haptics are even extending the world of gaming to visually impaired users. For example, the HapTech console utilizes a grid of vibrating motors to represent in-game objects and movements through directional vibrations, allowing players to experience the game world through touch.

Beyond training and accessibility, haptics are significantly enhancing gameplay mechanics. Imagine wielding a virtual sword and feeling the heat radiating from the blade as you forget it, or experiencing the satisfying pushback as you draw your bow in VR archery—these are just some of the possibilities offered by devices like the Sword of Elements, which incorporates heat and force feedback to create a multisensory gaming experience. Technologies like the Power of 2 (Po2) take it further, creating the illusion of movement using just two vibrating points on a controller. This allows for dynamic haptic sensations that add a new layer of interactivity to gameplay.

For an even more immersive experience, haptic vests and suits are also integrated into the gaming scene. These wearables are equipped with multiple motors strategically placed across the torso to generate a variety of sensations. Players can feel the wind whipping past them as they race through a virtual landscape or experience the chilling touch of rain during an in-game downpour. The Teslasuit takes this further by employing electro-stimulation to create a full-body haptic experience. This technology allows gamers to feel everything from the subtlest touch to a powerful impact, blurring the lines between the virtual and real worlds.

The influence of haptics extends beyond individual immersion. Haptic gaming chairs like the Cooler Master Motion 1 integrate haptic engines that move and vibrate in sync with the game. Imagine feeling the rumble of a tank rolling through the battlefield or the gentle sway of a virtual boat. These haptic chairs add another layer of immersion, creating a captivating gaming experience.

6.1.4 Chapter 4: Challenges of Designing Haptic Experiences

Chapter 4 explored the challenges of designing haptic experiences. Replicating realistic touch with haptic devices is challenging due to the complexity of human skin and the need to balance accuracy and affordability. High costs arise from the computational power and hardware complexity required to achieve high-fidelity tactile sensations. Effective haptic devices must balance stiffness, weight, and size to provide realistic force feedback while allowing smooth movement. They must also be capable of delivering strong and accurate sensations, which often come at a higher cost. Furthermore, the design process involves carefully selecting the actuator type, driving mechanism, and ability to deliver forces in multiple directions.

Haptic wearables must be adaptable, closely conforming to the user's body to deliver effective sensations. They must be compact and capable of rendering diverse feedback modalities like thermal sensations, pressure, vibration, texture, and skin stretch while being intuitive and requiring minimal user training.

Another pressing challenge in designing haptics is that haptic engineers lack robust tools and guidelines for creating haptic experiences. This lack of guidelines hinders collaboration and exploration. To address this limitation, new design methods and tools, like Feelix, a platform for authoring haptic experiences, are being developed.

This chapter also covered challenges specific to certain domains, such as healthcare, fitness applications, robots, space, and gaming. Applying haptics in healthcare faces challenges, including realistic feedback replication and affordability. Precise control, training for medical professionals, and real-time detection for conditions like over pronation are critical, along with balancing fidelity and cost in medical training simulators. Developing haptic systems for voice therapy and aiding lower-limb amputees also presents unique difficulties, requiring user-friendliness and personalization.

Haptic technology enhances user experiences in navigation and fitness tracking, but challenges include ensuring accurate feedback, tracking movements in dynamic environments, and balancing energy efficiency with feedback quality. Similarly, haptic technology in robotics offers intuitive interaction but faces challenges like replicating human touch, ensuring minimal latency, and balancing power efficiency with rich feedback.

Integrating haptic devices into space is challenging due to microgravity altering force perception and requiring new mechanisms to recreate tactile resistance. Space missions also face constraints on mass, power, and space, along with extreme conditions like temperature, radiation, and vacuum, conditions that demand specially crafted haptic devices. As such, standard electronics may not be suitable, which necessitates alternatives that can withstand these harsh environments.

In consumer electronics, challenges of integrating haptics include accurately rendering diverse tactile features like friction and textures, achieving consistent high-fidelity sensations across devices, and customizing for individual preference.

6.1.5 Chapter 5: Haptic Technology Adoption and Future Trends

Chapter 5 discussed the adoption and future trends of haptic technology. The haptic technology market, valued at USD 8 billion in 2022, is predicted to reach USD 25 billion by 2032, growing at a compounded annual growth rate of 11.05%. This growth is driven by smartphones, tablets, wearables, and the gaming industry. Adoption rates for haptic technology are assumed to depend on its economic utility, with high adoption rates in communications devices, gaming, and the automobile, lower rates in medical training and robotic surgery due to unfavorable cost–benefit trade-offs, and even more limited adoption in aerospace applications.

The evolution of haptic technology in personal communication devices showcases a journey from early pagers to advanced smartphones. Initially, pagers like the BellBoy and Motorola Pageboy II lacked vibration capabilities. Adoption of haptics took off in the late 1980s, with models like the Motorola Bravo Express Pager incorporating vibration alerts by 1991. This feature became standard in most pagers by 1995, driven by the need for discreet communication. Although pagers were phased out in 2018, their pioneering use of haptic feedback paved the way for adoption in other personal communication devices. In mobile phones, haptics began in 1997 with Nokia's "vibrating battery" for the Nokia 3110. A turning point came in 1999 with the Nokia 3210, the first to feature built-in vibration. This trend continued with smartphones like Apple's iPhone, which introduced advanced haptic technologies such as "3D Touch." Today, smartphones use Linear Resonant Actuators (LRAs) for precise haptic feedback, reflecting ongoing improvements.

The integration of haptic technology into laptops began in 2015 with Apple's launch of the first haptic-enabled laptop. However, here, the main reason to use haptics was to reduce moving parts in laptops to increase their durability. The Apple Taptic Engine replaced the traditional clickable trackpad with a solid glass trackpad, using an LRA to simulate clicks and taps, providing tactile responses to user interactions. Despite this innovative use, haptics in laptops remain limited to Apple devices, and this function so far has not extended to other areas, such as silent alerts.

The automotive industry is another pioneer of haptic technology. The main driver of adoption is to enhance safety and user experience. Early features like the Lane Keeping Assist (LKA) system used tactile feedback through the steering wheel to help maintain lane position without cluttering visual or audio channels.

Most high-end cars currently feature haptics in their steering wheels, pedals, or seats. These systems improve driver awareness, reduce stress, and reduce accident rates.

In cars, haptics also operate via an innovative use mode called "shared control," where driver actions trigger or inform continuous haptic feedback. This enhances the driving experience despite challenges like driver inattention and false positives.

Healthcare adoption rates also seem to be growing. In minimally invasive surgery, haptics enhance surgical precision by allowing surgeons to sense tissue texture. Haptics also improve medical training outcomes through more realistic feedback and rehabilitation outcomes by guiding patients in regaining motor skills. Advanced prosthetics with haptics can also give amputees a more natural sense of touch and control.

The adoption rate in aviation is also on the rise. Haptic technology enhances the effectiveness of pilot training by providing realistic control feedback and tactile anomaly detection. In military applications, haptic technology improves vehicle and weapon control. It is also used in teleoperation, allowing remote control of robots with tactile feedback.

Finally, this chapter points to several foresight tools and methods, such as scenario planning, horizon scanning, gap matrix analysis, and causal layered analysis, to help organizations anticipate and better prepare for future trends.

6.2 Final Remarks

This book has explored the exciting world of haptic technology, its fundamental principles, and its impact on a vast array of applications. It is important to note that haptic technology is still in its early phases of adoption in some fields and has reached saturation in others. Standardization is still developing for haptics. Thus, this leaves much room for innovation and exploration. However, it can also lead to compatibility issues between different haptic systems and ecosystems. Despite this lack of standards, the haptics industry is experiencing growth. It is expanding at a rate that outpaces the GDP growth rate. This reflects the increasing adoption rates of haptic technology across various applications. In addition, haptic technology has been integrated into various products, from medical devices to entertainment systems and everyday consumer products. As the technology matures and standardizes, we can expect adoption to increase.

Acknowledgements This research was funded by the joint UAEU-ZU grant no. R22021.